Nowhere Land

Journeys Through a Broken Nation

Ron Jacobs

Fomite
Burlington, VT

ISBN-13: 978-1-959984-45-0
Library of Congress Control Number: 2024931570

Fomite
58 Peru Street
Burlington, VT 05401
www.fomitepress.com
05-11-2024

Dedicated to Robert Niemi,
who spent his life trying to make sense
of those we call Americans

The bus was only half full. It was late February 2021 and quite chilly, as Vermont tends to be in February. We were all wearing COVID-19 masks and the heater on the bus was stifling. This was the first time I'd been on an intercity bus since the summer before COVID hit the States. My destination was Providence, Rhode Island. I had been through that city a few times in the past. Once was in the 1970s when I decided to hitch and take a Greyhound from Baltimore up to Boston. The other times involved trips from Cape Cod to Maryland when my son was a youngster. The weather was chilly when I arrived in Boston. After taking the T out to Braintree, I got into my now adult son Ian's car and he drove us back to Providence where he lives with his wife and son. There was still a fair amount of snow on the ground and the deciduous trees were bare, with nary a hint of the buds soon to arrive in spring.

A fellow around my age got on the bus in White River Junction, Vermont. He was carrying a bag of Milwaukee tools and a mid-size backpack. He sat across the aisle from me. He was a big guy, maybe six foot two and close to two hundred pounds. Short hair and a couple days beard on his face. As we rode through the desolate stretch of I-89 in New Hampshire between Hanover and Concord, he told me about various construction projects he had worked on in the area. One was a fish ladder near a small hydroelectric dam and another was a service station right off the highway. When we were going through the Tip O'Neill tunnel near Boston's South Station, he revealed he was taking the bus to Charlottesville, Virginia to visit his daughter and from there he was going to Arkansas to help build a couple houses for rich folk. I asked him if he was tired of working. He smiled and said yes and no. Yes because he didn't like taking jobs just because he needed money and no because he usually only took work he enjoyed. He told me his daughter kept telling him he needed to slow down so he could stop and smell the roses. However, whenever she said it, it made him feel older than he actually was. I told him I got it, but was glad I didn't have to punch a clock (so to speak) anymore. It wasn't long after our conversation ended that we were docked at the bus terminal. We bid each other the best as we got off the bus.

Two days later I was back at South Station, heading back to Vermont. I watched as each passenger in the line for the Lucky Star's noon bus to Manhattan was scanned by the driver with a handheld digital thermometer before stepping on to the boarding platform. Nobody resisted and nobody complained. The driver repeated his instructions over and over regarding masks and temperature readings in the time of COVID. The pandemic and its practices reshaping an ornery and angry nation. I wondered how those changes were being received in certain other parts of the nation, where public health seemed to have a different meaning than it did in my experience on the east coast of the United States.

The crowd at the train station near Burlington, Vermont was about average for a summer day, Forty-some folks gathered in the shade near the small depot only recently re-opened since COVID shut down so much of the world. It was early summer, 2022. The train had been running for a few months after more than a year when COVID precautions halted it, but passengers had to wait outside the closed depot no matter what the weather. The crowd was composed of grandparents heading to the suburbs of New York to visit the kids, travelers coming in from a hike on the Long Trail and going to the next destination on their trek. College students going to Amherst and its plethora of schools. The Winooski River runs along the track for much of the first thirty miles of the trip south. Sand, rocks and mud along its banks were visible, but its depth was fair; no drought yet in Vermont. The pastures, cornfields, and mountains overwhelm the senses in a manner that will be relished as the trip continues and concrete and asphalt replace what nature intended.

The change in the landscape is subtle as one travels from Burlington to the New York suburbs. The woods and fields of Vermont are only occasionally interrupted by small and smaller towns along the track. Indeed, it isn't until one is south of Greenfield, Massachusetts that industrial structures and houses began to dominate the scenery. Even then, there are still enough woods on both sides of the train a passenger can ignore the impending aesthetic dissonance that describes the dystopian reality of much of the eastern seaboard. A similar phenomenon can be seen in the passengers boarding at each stop. The styles become more urban. Fades in the haircuts, a brutal razor's edge taken to the skull in an attempt to reflect or blend in to an urban architecture defined by angle. Conversations become louder and one cannot help but hear personal issues they might rather not. It's almost like riding a city bus where neighbors play out their disputes and their affairs, teenagers their loves and nonsense, and people complain about the weather no matter what it is. By the time the train is in the tunnel that leads into Manhattan's Penn Station, the ride is more like a ride on the D Train heading north from West 4th than an interstate train collecting and dispersing its human cargo up and down the coast.

Certain towns along the way take one back to how it used to be. Bellows Falls, VT is one such place. The waters of the Connecticut river are slowed by the walls that fence it in through the town, one can almost hear the water wheels turning crushing grain or powering looms. The industrial revolution that moved New Englanders off the farms and out of the shacks to fill the pockets of the bankers down river with more money then the workers would ever see in a dozen lifetimes of wage slavery. It turned the towns upside down, fed the tavern owners, freed the children from the structures of home and church and replaced them with the oppression of capitalism and its measly rewards the bosses call a payday—a ritual they begrudgingly go along with.

I don't want to mislead the reader. The trip through Vermont and the parts of Massachusetts before Greenfield certainly have a good share of nature's beauty. But, as is the case anywhere humans have set up community, there's a fair amount of denatured ugliness, too. Gravel quarries and landfills hidden from the civilized outposts that demand these blights. Junked cars, junk food joints and junkyards, smokestacks beyond the corn. Corn that gets taller the further south one travels; corn that represents our societal addiction to sugar and beef. Corn syrup and silage is what the pilgrims wrought. Maybe the Pequot emissaries knew what they were doing when they let the Puritans take their corn. John Winthrop sent his repressed militia off to massacre the Pequot; subsequently the murdered have their revenge on the white folks that followed. I'm reminded of a routine titled "Temporarily Humboldt County" by the psychedelic comedy group Firesign Theater which includes the line: "We discovered corn, now we can make whiskey!"

When considering the genocide of the indigenous people in northern America, especially in its early days in New England, it wasn't the soldiers' attacks that presented the greatest obstacle to indigenous survival, but the settlers who followed. After all, soldiers left, once their mission demanded they go elsewhere, allowing indigenous nations like the Abenaki to use the lands once the soldiers had moved on. Settlers stayed, building homes, establishing farms and fighting to keep them on lands taken from their previous residents. Despite the best intentions and furious fighting of the indigenous, their fate was often sealed. When the newcomer's intention is genocide, the future has few question marks for those whose lives are slated for elimination.

I've been taking this Amtrak train from Burlington, Vermont to Baltimore, Maryland since I first moved to Vermont in 1992. It's a twelve hour ride if everything is running on time. There used to be two trains a day when the trip began in Montreal. Sometime right after the events of 9/11 the Montreal to Vermont stretch of the trip was canceled. It has yet to return. The journey takes one through the Green Mountains of Vermont, their slopes filled with mostly deciduous trees; oaks and various kinds of maples. The autumn hillsides are full of oranges and reds, even purples, as the leaves change their colors before falling to the earth to eventually be buried by winter snow. Often several feet of snow. The train winds through Vermont, taking about four hours to get from Burlington at the northwest corner of the state to White River Junction in its southeast corner. The town of Burlington is a modern mix of college students, money-chasers, workers in the tourist industry, blue-collar workers keeping everything going and repaired as best they can, and tech and educational types. When I first moved there in 1992, Bernie Sanders was just finishing his first term as a congressman after having been Burlington's Mayor for most of the previous decade. The other town of White River Junction is the site of a VA hospital, a classic New England downtown, fast food joints, small farmers and people on their way to another part of the state. In 1992, White River Junction was in a part of the state that was quite conservative, both culturally and politically. Fiscal conservatism and a distrust of counterculture types—hippies, punks, gays, whatever—seemed the dominant consciousness. Like much of Vermont, that is no longer the case in 2022.

When Vermont first began considering civil unions for gay couples, White River Junction and other more traditional and rural areas of Vermont were the sites of numerous signs painted on barns decrying the move (billboards are illegal in Vermont). Mostly, those signs said "Take Back Vermont!" It was never exactly clear to me who or what Vermont needed to be taken back from or to, but that was their slogan and they stuck with it until the bitter end, when the gay marriage legislation passed. One can still see the slogan painted on a barn here and there. The paint is fading; one hopes the intolerance did too. Despite the fears of the more reactionary elements of that campaign, Vermonters didn't come out of the closet by the thousands, and neither did gay hordes invade the state. Sure, it seemed a few more LBGT folks moved north from the east coast megalopolis, but life went on pretty much as before. People adjusted, proving once again that fear is usually born from ignorance. When it came time to pass gay marriage legislation, not even the small Christian right churches made much of a stink. Nowadays, those churches are slightly larger, and much more confident. They certainly inject their venom into the conversation; some of their members have attacked school boards around Critical Race Theory and books about trans people, both things they fear for reasons probably not even known to most of them. Fortunately, this isn't Texas, and their attacks have been met with vocal and (unlike the bigots) intelligent responses. Protests by parents and students are sending these types calling themselves Christian back to their pews in their churches of the holy rollers.

Don't get me wrong. There are racists and other kinds of bigots in Vermont. As a general rule, they don't make it super obvious by using the n word when they're talking about people whose skin isn't white, but they might as well. There's always been plenty of code words available for the racist who doesn't want to get his ass kicked and the appearance of Trumpism has created a lot more of those words and phrases. Also, as the state of Vermont has become less white, at least in the cities, the racists have become more open in their expression. There are a few individuals who practice shooting their weapons at so-called right-wing militia camps in the woods. Still, it's not Texas with its hate-filled politicians still pretending Juneteenth never happened or even Maryland, where many a racist hides behind their suburban lawn. Or doesn't hide at all, but proudly broadcasts their bigotry.

White River Junction is a bigger town than it was the first few years I went through there. It's still more conservative culturally and politically, but it can no longer be considered reactionary, especially when it comes to social and cultural phenomena. A few larger motel chains have built franchises right off Interstate 89 and a few more chain restaurants have set up shop nearby. Once one leaves the old downtown, it looks more like New Hampshire just north of Massachusetts, than picture-book Vermont, but then again so do the suburban areas surrounding Burlington. The usual suspects run their shops in both places: Subway, MacDonald's, Hampton Inn, Best Western. The train stops there for a couple minutes and meanders its way south through the center of Massachusetts.

Greenfield is the first stop in what they call the Pioneer Valley—a moniker with its multitude of meanings. Explorers and Indian killers and hippies escaping from the cities and the cops come quickly to mind. The valley hosts several food co-ops and music festivals. There's even a Buddhist center that moves one closer to the gods if one allows oneself to take that trip. Greenfield and other towns are conveniently within an hour or so of Amherst, Northampton and their colleges with the youthful culture that defines such towns. The Berkshires rise up in the west, promising an isolation treasured by many New Englanders past and present; famous and otherwise. The politics to the west are a bit more conservative than in Boston or Burlington, but in today's USA, where Nazi maniacs sit in state legislatures in its south and central lands, the fear of liberals keeps the bulk of the fascist cretins away.

I watch as we pull into Springfield, a city searching for its meaning ever since industry mostly pulled out. A couple of young guys with dreadlocks—one white and one Black—get on the train, wait until the conductor scans the ticket on their cellular devices then moves to his place in the food car where he waits for the next stop. The two young bloods step into the space between cars, pull out their vape pens and inhale. When they open the car door and step back into the car, a slight whiff of legal marijuana drifts through the space. Nobody looks up. Nobody gives a fuck. I recalled  riding Greyhound buses in the 1970s across the country. Back then the bathroom window opened and we would go back there to take a hit or two on a joint and blow the smoke out the window. You could still smoke tobacco on the bus in the back couple of seats.

Drinking alcohol was not allowed, but most drivers didn't care. I do remember a guy getting tossed out in the middle of acres of cornfields in Nebraska when he refused to put his bottle away. The tee-totaling Christian driver with the big cross hanging around his neck was not messing around. He made his point. It was one of the more sober Greyhound journeys I ever took. I was heading to Oakland and did not want end to up on the side of the road. That driver drove us all the way to Denver. The new driver was less worried about people sipping on a bottle as long as they didn't get rowdy.

The legalization of weed is one of the best things to come out of the Sixties. Not the best thing—that was the music and the more open attitudes about appearance, gender and sexual adventures—but legalization was certainly number two in my book after music. Now that that time is in the distance, I don't necessarily regret the days here and there I spent in jail and court for smoking illegal pot, but damn it would have been a better life without those times. Of course, when I was busted and found myself in a city jail somewhere and had no idea if I would be getting out or going deeper into the system, I was scared and angry. I can only imagine what was going through the heads of those with darker skin in the same situation. I usually got out within a couple days. The same would not be true for non-whites, then or now. Being behind bars is never fun; not when it is happening, nor in retrospect.

After Springfield, the scenery outside the train becomes more suburban and then more urban. The young men with the vape pens have chilled out and are watching videos on their devices. As one rides into Connecticut, names of towns from John Cheever novels are announced by the conductors. So many of the new passengers seem to be living a twenty-first century version of that Bullet Park world — suburban despair now with expensive cellular devices and less Valium, thanks to the pharmaceutical industry's neverending search for the ultimate soma drug. Million dollar houses and one-hundred thousand dollar cars. More people get on the train than off going into Manhattan, while the opposite is true when it heads back north.

By now the train is full. Every single seat has a body in it. The scheduled stops at the university towns in Massachusetts saw a few folks get on, but it's in New Haven, where a monolith of a police station stands across from the train station, it's brick walls a foreboding presence, that the train reaches capacity. The police station's windows are almost non-existent, just a few rectangles of bulletproof glass reminiscent of gun apertures in prisons. The building is quite clearly designed to be the occupiers' defense against the proletariat and its mostly nascent antagonism towards the powerful elements the police protect—Yale University, defense industry affiliates, climate destroying corporations with a social conscience smaller than the head of a pin and everything else that comes with the university-industrial complex. It reminds me of the forts the US Army built to kill native peoples as the US settler invasion pushed westward across the North American continent.

The environs of Stamford, Connecticut are next. The bourgeoisie's boats float in the marinas and their luxury vehicles zoom down the highway. Nothing affects them except for maybe a dip in the stock marker or an attorney's bill for their adult child's fuckups. The adolescents take the train into the city, some to shop and some to get high; some to take classes and some to hang with the gutter punks wherever they hang these days. The cool kids dress the part, and the rest look like the twenty-first century version of the cast of *The Breakfast Club*. Their parents look like a graying version of the same. I can't help but hope the youngsters reject the lifestyle their parents embraced and go rogue. They don't need to commit class suicide and join some revolution, but even telling their parents they don't want that 70,000 dollar car means something, I suppose. We all know the planet's burning. The question is how much more fuel will we throw into the fire. From where I sit, it seems the answer is that no one in power is actually willing to put restrictions on the quantity. We are hell-bound hellhounds on a highway to hell.

It was the two trips described above that got me thinking about some more involved journeys and this book. I had not really traveled further than from Vermont to Washington, DC since the COVID scenario began. Most of those trips were to help take care of my ailing father, who died in February 2021. The last time I had been out to the west coast of the US was in 2018, when a friend and I went to California for a week. Shit must have changed out there. I know it has on the eastern side of the land mass. I knew in my heart it was time to hit the road. I felt it in my soul, in my boots, my brain and my veins. Some general plans began to coalesce.

First, though, let me tell you a bit more about the town in Vermont where I live these days. Ever since the US military's F-35

death planes came to the nearby airport, the skies are ripped apart, the roar of the multimillion dollar engines piercing not just eardrums but the brains of myself and those who reside around me. In the fall, the honks of the geese flying south are drowned out by those engines. In the summer even the bluejays hide, their squawks quieted. All year round, dogs and cats hide under sofas and beds. The rest of the time (when the killer jets aren't flying), I can hear birds; crows conversing in their raucous manner, the occasional dove cooing or the gull screeching. The smaller birds tweet and chirp most days when winter's cold and dark hasn't chased them inside or far away. A few wild animals traverse this urban landscape. I've seen opossum, raccoons, rabbits, even a red fox or two. The coyotes howl from a more wooded area perhaps five miles away and the deer stay near the river a few hundred meters from my home.

Back to those death planes. Vermont is a strange place to base the things. Not because it doesn't have its hand in the pocket of the war machine. In fact, General Dynamics, the company that built and sold one of the first weapons of mass destruction — the Gatling gun — used to be headquartered in Burlington. The reason it's strange to have those noisy and deadly planes in Vermont's skies is because it would seem there were better places to base them. Wide, open places or places next to the ocean, perhaps. But, the money was too good for the Vermont politicians to ignore. Indeed, Senator Patrick Leahy, who is now retired, begged for the damn things. Of course, the media's remembrances of that senator's tenure in the Senate and what they call public service didn't spend much time discussing his role in bringing the death planes to Vermont. Nor did they recall his role as a federal prosecutor in arresting protesters against the US invasion of Cambodia and the murders at Kent State at the US Federal Building in Burlington, Vermont in 1970. He was a true servant of the state. I curse him every time the win-

13

dows rattle and the cats hide. Then I thank the gods I don't live in a land where the F-35s' mission is considerably more deadly.

Despite the military madness described above, the Burlington, Vermont area is quite beautiful. The waves of Lake Champlain splash along its western border, the Adirondack Mountains can be seen in the distance on the lake's other side. The housing ranges from old Victorians divided into apartments to classic New England workforce housing—two stories, two units — mostly located in the oldest part of the small city. More suburban enclosures make up the bulk of the rest of the residents' homes. Of course, there are newer multifamily units built in the 1970s and after, along with dozens of condominium and apartment edifices constructed since 2010. The downtown area is currently the home of several dozen shops and restaurants catering to tourists, college students and residents, in that order. Outdoor sports retail chains come and go from the downtown district. Despite its Vermont version of crass commercialism, it can be a vibrant and even charming place on certain days.

Winooski, which is across a river with the same name from Burlington, has less apparent money. In fact, it is still mostly a working class town, referring to its beginnings (as far as white folks settling there anyhow) as a mill town. The bulk of the mill workers were of French descent and that history is reflected in the saints in the Catholic churches and many of the area's family names. Like Burlington, Winooski's downtown hosts many restaurants and bars catering to student and tourist populations. The area's small size and decent public transit system makes getting around easy, even for those who complain  about it. Although there is gentrification going on, it seems to be occurring at a slower pace than other places I have been. The Winooski river's name means onion and is a word taken from the Abenaki, who inhabited and hunted the land now called Vermont and southern Quebec before the French and British came. A type of onion known as ramps grow wild along certain stretches of the river. The first I actually ever heard the vegetables called ramps was in Asheville, North Carolina; another mountainous region with many similarities to the Green Mountains in Vermont, beside the fact they are all part of the Appalachians. In fact, a woman who regularly brought her family to the library where I worked once brought me a small pie made with ramps, chicken and gravy. It was delicious.

The first time I headed west was in December 1977. Summer that year began when I returned from Munich, Germany in May. With a pocketful of money I had earned working at a cafeteria on a US Army base, I landed in Baltimore and headed for a liquor store. Within a week, I had a couple ounces of Colombian marijuana, a sheet of blotter acid with R. Crumb's Mr. Natural printed on each perforated square, and tickets to see the Grateful Dead and Little Feat in successive weeks at the Baltimore Civic Center.

That beginning set the tone for the season. I was invited to a shindig at a farm outside of Charleston, West Virginia. Rock bands, Rebel Yell whiskey, a few hundred folks and two barbecued pigs in a pit. There was coleslaw and potato salad too. And baked beans. A guy who called himself Mad Dog befriended me for the weekend and we had a hollering time. My understanding was that the farm was owned by a guy who was part of a group that smuggled weed into Key West and up the coast. He was making a lot of money moving a few hundred pounds a week. Later that summer when weed was hard to find, he helped us all out with a pound he had stashed just for such a time.

The first Saturday in December a friend and I hopped on a bus to Mobile, Alabama. Snow was beginning to fall. Back then Greyhound had a deal that let you ride as far as you could in twenty-four hours for twenty-five bucks. Our trip took us from Maryland to Mobile. It was early evening when we arrived in Mobile and we were hungry. My friend, whom I'll call Dawn, grew up in Macon, Georgia. She knew the south, its pleasures and its ways, its racism and its rationales. We chowed down on some fried chicken and greens, bought a six pack of Dixie beer, found a cheap motel where we stole a couple tokes each of a joint in the bathroom of our room, careful to blow the smoke up into the ceiling fan away into the night, turned on the television and made love. Southern nights.

The bathroom window was open. The salty smell of the Gulf of Mexico informed my dreams. Oil tankers emitted their own odor, occasionally overriding the natural smell of saltwater and ocean decay. Seaweed, fish and diesel fuel had me thinking I was adrift on a shrimp boat or some other craft designed to stay afloat on mother ocean. The next morning came early, with Dawn in my arms. After showering, we headed out. Breakfast was a couple eggs over easy, coffee and a pork product. Ninety-nine cents each plus tip. The waitress—a thirty-something brunette with blue eyes and legs that never seemed to end—told us how to get to the closest entrance to Interstate 10. She told Dawn to be safe and we headed down the road. Time to try our luck at hitchhiking.

Our first ride came quickly. Two white guys going back to a shipyard in Pascagoula, Mississippi. Their weekend was winding down. Dawn and I hadn't been in the car ten minutes when the guy riding shotgun fired up a joint. The miles flew past like the smoke from our lungs. Both the driver and his buddy were Alabama boys who knew each other from childhood, joined the Army together, went to Vietnam and came back at the same time. Both had been mechanics at an Army motor pool in Saigon and neither saw any real combat. When they got back to the States, neither thought they would end up back in their Alabama hometown. But, like the driver said, shit happens. You try and make it in California, and you don't. You go to another city like Chicago and you fuck that up too, so you go home. Robert Frost said that home is a place where when you go there they have to take you in. Then you run into an old girlfriend from high school, fuck around and get her pregnant. That ends up defining at least the next fifteen or twenty years. He continued his story. It was half lament and half celebration. His buddy took a pint of Southern Comfort out of the glove box and passed it around. The landscape flashed by. The impression I am left with was a lot of small pine, green vegetation and wetlands. Occasionally a heron looked up from its fishing task and flew off. The sky was as blue as a sky can be. Or at least as blue as I've ever seen one. Our conversation was mostly about music. When we discovered the two men were fans of Little Feat—something that didn't happen that often—we began discussing their most recent release and what seemed like Lowell George's growing distance from the band. When we arrived in Pascagoula, they showed us downtown. A small fountain was somewhere near the middle of it. A couple of alligators lay still in the water, their snouts in the air. We said thanks and goodbye. Our goal was to make it to New Orleans by nightfall.

We stood on the side of the entrance ramp onto I-10. Cars went by, and a convoy of Army trucks. GIs sitting in the back of the ¾ ton vehicles flashed us peace signs. Eventually they all drove on to whatever exercise they were going to play out in the bayous and woods of Mississippi. Just as a light rain began to fall, a small two-door hatchback pulled over. We ran to the vehicle and jumped in. The driver was a woman around our age. Dawn jumped into the front passenger seat and I jumped into the back. Dawn and the driver began to talk and I fell asleep. The driver was a salesperson that sold stuff to hotels and motels. She was around our age and was listening to an Allman Brothers cassette when we hopped in the car. When I woke up we were in New Orleans parked in front of a Holiday Inn. After a quick conversation and a goodbye to the driver, Dawn and I decided to spend the night at the hotel. We got a few stares when we walked in with our backpacks and sleeping bags, but it was New Orleans, and nobody asked us to leave. They took our money and gave us a key to our room. After dropping everything in the room, I went outside to find food and beer. Dawn stayed behind.

What I remember was drinking a few beers, eating some kind of fish sandwich with fries, and falling asleep while watching the television. The next state we would be traversing would be Texas. I was about to discover what Bob Wills meant when he sang about miles and miles of Texas. The last time I had even been in the state was when I was a toddler. At the time, it wasn't considered to be the bulwark of the Confederacy on the other side of the Mississippi. In fact, thanks to musicians like Willie Nelson, Townes Van Zandt, Jerry Jeff Walker and the rest, Texas had a certain hippie outlaw reputation. Add to that the dope smuggling subculture, one of the best underground newspapers known as The Rag, and the city of Austin's Guadalupe Street, and Texas had as much cred in the dying counterculture of 1977 as Cambridge or Venice Beach did at the time. After all, the creeping consumerism of the mainstream had neutralized a fair number of freak and hippie communities, turning them into gentrified ghettos. It wasn't like the counterculture had gone mainstream, but that enough of its adherents got snookered into buying shit instead of changing it.

My mention of Townes van Zandt reminds me of a later Texas journey where I ended up at a music festival near Kerrville. It was one of those hitchhikes where I just went wherever the rides took me. It was in the early 1980s. I had left Austin a day earlier, heading mostly west on 290. A couple of longhaired Texans picked me up and said they were heading to the festival. I was aware of the festival, but it was not necessarily my destination. We got near the festival grounds and the driver asked if I had any money for a ticket. I said no and he said they would let me off at a place where it was easiest to sneak in. I said thanks and hopped out where he told me to. It was around midnight. I wandered around for a little while until I felt it was a good time to sneak in. I got through the fence and headed towards some trailers. They happened to be where the performers hung out. I walked up acting like I kind of belonged there, set my pack down and sat on it. A skinny guy with long hair and a big bottle of wine looked up from the steps in front of the trailer he was sitting on. He passed me the bottle. I took a drink and passed it back. We did that silently for a few passes. Then he started talking. It took me a minute or two before I recognized the voice. It was Townes Van Zandt, I was certain. We kept on drinking until the bottle was gone. I had one hell of a headache when I woke up a few hours later right next to my pack. The sun was hot as hell already.

The next morning, Dawn and I got some breakfast, turned in our key and walked to an entrance onto Interstate 10. The weather was reasonably warm. We got a ride as we got near the entrance ramp. If I recall correctly, it was a tractor-trailer and it was going to Houston. It was our first ride with a trucker and only the second or third one I had ever received in five years of hitchhiking. Up until sometime in the 1980s, many if not most truckers were independent operators. Nowadays, most are hired by a company or corporation that either leases out their trucks to individual drivers, or the drivers are regular employees of the corporation whose goods they are moving. The biggest difference in terms of hitchhiking (not that anyone hitches in the United States anymore) is that many of the drivers before the contractual situation changed had insurance which didn't make picking up hitchhikers a violation of the policy. Now, even independents have clauses written into their policies that forbid the practice.

The driver this time was a talkative guy around forty years old. He liked Dawn a lot, but was gentlemanly to her. He shared a box of donuts with us, gave us each a couple white crosses (black market Dexedrine) and talked a lot. His trailer was empty and he was driving it to Houston where he would trade it for a full trailer. Then, he said, he would drive that trailer to Tampa where he would pick up another full trailer and drive it to Houston. His eight track collection was pretty eclectic: everything from George Jones to Al Green to Pink Floyd's *Dark Side of the Moon*. As we traveled, he told stories about the country we were passing through. Some were tales about his personal experience in such and such a town while others were history lessons. Andrew Jackson, killing indigenous people and the like. When we got to Houston, he pulled into a parking lot near the depot where he was scheduled to trade his empty trailer for a full one. We got out and headed to a diner for a meal. He joined us after taking care of his business. It began to lightly rain. Then, he offered us the use of his cab if we wanted to sleep. Before I could think of a polite way to say no, Dawn took him up on the offer. We spent three or four hours in the cab. Dawn slept and I read one of the books I brought along. I think it was *Desolation Angels* by Kerouac. The driver was doing his own thing. The rain stopped and Dawn woke up. We ate some tacos and waited for the driver to return. When he did, we bid our goodbyes, took our gear and headed to another entrance ramp about a quarter mile from where the truck was parked. We didn't get a ride until an hour or so after dark.

While we waited for a ride, the Houston police paid us a visit. Although they came off rather menacingly at first, they calmed down after running our identification through their system and finding no warrants. Dawn conversed with one cop while the other told me about a better ramp a couple miles away. It was in a better part of town is what he said. I told him thanks, they got back into their cruiser and within five minutes a car pulled over and told us to hop in. We did.

It took us all the way to Austin. On the way we smoked a few joints and drank a six pack of Lone Star. When we ran out of beer we were in the middle of nowhere about two hours from Austin and just getting into what passes for hills in Texas. The driver pulled into a Circle K convenience store so we could pee and get more beer. When I brought the beer to the counter to pay, the clerk—a Mexican woman—told me she couldn't sell beer after 1 AM. On the way to return the beer to the refrigerator I dropped the six-pack and broke a bottle. She went ahead and let me buy the beer. By the time we had finished the beer we were on the outskirts of Austin. Crystal Gayle was singing "Don't It Make My Brown Eyes Blue?" on the Top 40 radio station. The driver dropped us off on Guadalupe Street and drove off. Dawn and I went looking for a cheap hotel. We were all fairly drunk, despite the handful of white crosses he shared with us in the Circle K parking lot.

The hotel we found was on a street right off Guadalupe. Most of the tenants were single folks of all ages. My guess was that it was a place where the manager rented out rooms for months at a time, took his tenants' rents off the top of their disability and welfare checks and ignored most of what they did. We took off our clothes and fell asleep immediately. The sun was rising as were settling. We slept like logs until evening. The shower gave us enough hot water to take a quick shower together. It was cold in the room and outside. Getting dressed, we talked about getting some real Mexican food and some more Lone Star. Heading out the door of the hotel, the manager told us about a bar two blocks away that had good Mexican food, Lone Star beer, and his friend's country rock band on the bill. It was a great evening. The next morning we were going back on the road.

We were halfway through Texas and it seemed like we had just begun. As we stood with our thumbs out and our bedrolls by our feet all we could see was land and sky. Fortunately, before the feeling got too desolate, we got a ride with a guy driving a beat-up pickup truck. He fired up a joint of some okay weed as soon as we got in the cab. The weather was cold, not more than twenty degrees. The sun was hidden by clouds and it smelled like snow. We were probably on the interstate for two hours when the driver, who called himself Red, said he needed to stop by his place. I looked at Dawn, shrugged and said alright. I had no idea where the hell he was taking us because there was nothing but range surrounded by barbed wire all around us. No buildings, no towns, no trees not even any steers, sheep or other livestock. Hopefully, the hitchhiking gods were smiling on us.

About five minutes after I gave my assent, he took a sharp left onto a single lane road that went slowly up a slight hill. About five miles in I saw a single wide trailer in the distance. A motorcycle was next to it and a dog came running down the road when we were a quarter mile or so away. It was a big old hound dog, ears flapping as it ran and barked. Red parked his truck, said hello to his dog and invited us in. The temperature had dropped and the wind was whipping up a bit. We went inside, he started a fire in his stove and set some tamales wrapped in foil on the top. While the tamales heated up, he told us he was a caretaker for some rancher who owned all the land for miles around. Got a trailer and three hundred fifty bucks a month to ride around and make sure the barbed wire wasn't cut and in the summer when the cattle were around, he had to keep them inside the fences. Said he'd been doing it since he left the Army in 1971. There'd been a couple of women in his life, but mostly it was him, his dogs, his pot plants, and the comfort women of Austin, as he put it. He continued, telling us that he usually grew about six pounds of weed every season; kept a couple pounds for himself, and sold the rest to a guy who worked at Armadillo World Headquarters, a famous bar in Austin. He brewed some strong hobo coffee, gave us a dozen tamales and took us back to the highway. We said our goodbyes. He went back up his road and we stuck out our thumbs again.

It was a desolate stretch of road. In two hours not more than ten vehicles went by. A couple stopped but were only going a couple miles up the road so we begged off. It was still early afternoon. The view was stunning and the temperature was around freezing. When the sun broke through, it felt warm. The Texas shadows turned the chaparral purple, brown and red. The sun turned it gold for an instant here and there. The tamales were delicious and the thermos of coffee kept us warm. Still, I didn't really want to sleep out in the open in that particular spot on that particular night. The afternoon slipped away. We were gathering some wood for a small fire when a big old Ford four-door screeched to a stop, a tall fellow with short hair combed back like Johnny Cash got out and yelled hey. I walked slowly over. He offered a ride and a place to stay for the night. The next town, he said, was about thirty miles away. We could stop, get some beer, he could call his wife from the general store to let her know we were coming and we could settle in. By this time Dawn was standing next to me. I looked at her and we said yeah, sure, thanks.

He picked up a couple cases of Lone Star, some tortillas, milk, and whiskey at the store in town. Then we headed out to his place. It was a rambler type house with a few rooms added on. I understood why when we went inside. There were six kids, a couple of dogs, his wife and her sister living there. It was loud, like one of those television shows where everyone's friendly and unassuming, only it was real. And it stayed that way all evening while we ate enchiladas, drank beer and whiskey, watched television and played cards. When I started falling asleep, his wife offered Dawn and me their bed. We said no, but they insisted. As my mind wandered off to dreamland I thought about Lyndon Baines Johnson. I was deep in the heart of Texas, after all.

Since we started our journey, Dawn and I had been part of too many conversations to count. We talked about music and we talked about films. We discussed the ocean and how shrimping worked. We listened while shipyard workers told us about building boats and we wondered aloud about the meaning of a coyote's howl. We hooped and hollered when the liquor cheered us up. One thing that had never come up was politics. Jimmy Carter was in the White House, and Richard Nixon was drinking scotch in California plotting his revenge. The rest of the country seemed to be taking a break. From the revolution or reality, it didn't matter.

We were back on the road in the morning. California was closer than it was further and closer than it was yesterday. The temperature was back in the forties and the sun foretold a warmer day ahead. We cleaned up the rest of the enchiladas and our most recent friend took us into town, where he hooked us up with a ride. It was with a man in the Air Force whose leave was ending. He was going back to Phoenix after seeing his girlfriend and family for a few days. Tally ho.

The Texas landscape zoomed by. Dawn was sleeping in the back seat of the airman's van while he and I talked about everything from the Beatles to Burger King, and from the Air Force to the Marines. He had enlisted for a four-year stint and was in his second year. He liked the fact that he was being trained to be an aircraft mechanic and figured that's what he would do when he got out. Already, his commanding officer was trying to convince him to re-enlist. I did my best to convince him otherwise. His girlfriend, who he hoped would become his fiance, wasn't sure one way or the other. She was tired of the small Texas town we had just left but unsure about pretty much everything else. That's how the driver put it, anyhow. When a radio station played "Hey Jude" he told me it was his favorite Beatles' song. I told him mine was "Get Back". We were around the same age.

By the time we got to Phoenix (that's a song, too), Dawn was awake. The driver dropped us off at a small roadside motel next to a Mexican restaurant. We gathered our things, traded addresses and bid farewell. Dawn and I paid ten bucks for a room, set down our stuff in the room and went over to the restaurant where we ate burritos and got drunk. Then we went back to the motel and made love. The desert sun woke us at six the next morning. The room was tinged in gold. We packed up and walked a couple of miles into town where we ate huevos rancheros at the first open restaurant we saw, paid the bill and hit the road. We stood on a main street heading out of Phoenix. Orange trees full of fruit everywhere. Dawn and I picked a half dozen. We were barely through when a police cruiser that had been parked across the street pulled up. The cop inside got out and walked over to us, his hand on his holstered gun. We were clean (as in no illegal substances on our persons), so I wasn't too concerned. He probably just wanted to make sure we were heading out of town. Little did we know that it was illegal to pick oranges from the trees on public lands in Phoenix. We apologized. Don't eat them, he said. They're poisoned. Dawn was ready to jump in his face, but I reminded her it wasn't the cop who poisoned them. If they were poisoned, that is.

Our next ride was a long one. The driver, who sold raw crystals and unpolished gems that he mined and traded to dealers and jewelers, took us all the way to Palm Springs. As he told us stories of seedy sex in Palm Springs bedrooms, the desert rolled by. Cacti of all sizes here and there, hot sun reflecting off the sand and waves of heat rising to distort the air. Tumbling tumbleweeds even. I don't know if he was trying to impress us with his sex stories—some of which featured him but were mostly gossip about movie stars and their toys. The weather was much warmer. No more temperatures below freezing for Dawn and me.

We got out of the gem dealer's van in front of a McDonald's. It wasn't five minutes before the manager came out and told us to move. I found it strange he was dressed up like a maître d'. Dawn laughed when he asked us to move. It's a fuckin' McDonald's is what she told him. I looked inside and realized that this McDonald's had waiters. We laughed and moved on. Then we laughed some more. Mercedes and Rolls Royces drove by, not even seeing us. Our ride came via a surfer guy driving a Dodge Charger. He took us all the way to Huntington Beach and talked about surfing most of the way. We had friends from back east in Huntington Beach. Someday soon, it would be known as the birthplace of a certain kind of hardcore punk music. When we got there, it was just a beach town with way too many cops and John Birchers trying to figure out how to keep the youth under control and the Blacks and Latinos out. Our friends would move soon to another Orange County town further inland. It was even more nondescript and considerably more intolerant of people who didn't fit a certain mold that's probably best described as Southern California white man. If you've ever read cartoonist R. Crumb's classic comic of social satire titled "Adventures of Whiteman" you'll know exactly what I mean. If not, you might get it anyhow. I was not amused.

After a month of partying and being harassed on the beach by a variety of different authorities—lifeguards with steroid muscles, cops in shorts with tear gas guns on their belts, and cops in helicopters—Dawn and I said our goodbyes and headed north to Berkeley. It was early in the morning when we put our thumbs out. By evening we were walking up University Avenue in Berkeley. We got ourselves a room with our dwindling funds and headed to Telegraph Avenue, one of the final fronts in the battle for America's hearts and minds. It was a battle the peaceniks, freaks, and radicals were losing. Overwhelmed by the sheer power of the establishment's money and guns against our predominantly nonviolent and relatively poor numbers, the end of the Sixties revolution was closer than I thought. Some people got co-opted into the capitalist cash-hoarding machine, some went to work to support children that had occurred, some lost their minds, some were in prison mostly for weed, and some were just too far gone. Telegraph Avenue was the focal point of the outpost that was Berkeley. Dawn and I were ready to jump in the deep end and see what kind of shit was going on.

In the weeks to come I would get busted for weed, harassed frequently by the cops, Dawn and I would find a place to live in East Oakland, and eat a lot of LSD. Living on the street was an education with little room for mistakes. One fuckup could put you in prison for awhile. The cops who patrolled the streets of Berkeley made it their business to fuck with longhairs and other poor people, especially those with darker skin. Of course, this defines the work of cops in most urban areas if adjusted for the changes in hairstyles. The difference in Berkeley was the ongoing presence of the counterculture, which served to widen the net cast by the cops. In comparison, suburbia was a piece of cake. Cake in the sense that it was full of sparkles and nutritionally empty. It was a place I had no desire to return to. Suburbia was, after all, a cake whose main ingredients were greed, fear, and trying to keep up to standards determined not by kindness but its opposite. And lots of schlock. Neon nonsense blinking out its message to buy buy buy and sell your soul to the owner of the Madison Avenue voice in the television set. Cover the green grass with indoor malls and pretend the air would stay clean all on its own. Don't forget your car payments and dentist appointments. Or the scrip for the anti-depressants.

When I began the journeys that inspire this book, I (half) jokingly referred to them as my journey into the bowels of the American dream. You know how after a meal of rich foods like lobster or crab and a few pints your gastrointestinal system tends to be in a state of disruption? That's the state of the US of A in the twenty-first century. You might take an antacid to settle things down or you might just end up wrestling with your insides. However, no matter what happens, shit's going to come out in the end. My original intention was to take one long journey and write. As it turned out—and in a perfect example of the financial situation of most residents of the USA, I couldn't afford such a trip. I had to go back home after each jaunt and earn money for the next journey. As Gilbert Shelton's underground cartoon character, Oat Willie, used to say, onward through the fog. The fog of poverty, the fog of war, the fog of creeping fascism. The fog of modern life and its many disenchantments. And its many enchantments.

Contemplating this, the country appears as both a sewer and a land of enchantment. Individual places can be both at the same time. The McMansions certain folks live in are often gratuitous displays of fleeting wealth that represent an obsequious greed their residents might not even consciously know exists within them. A row house in an ungentrified part of Baltimore is often more likely to possess a genuine sense of home. This is a nation that considers the concerns of billionaire ogres in their castles to be more important than mothers and their babies, and protects guns more than schoolchildren. A nation founded to defend and promote its early vision of capitalism on the backs of African slaves and their descendants, indentured servants, and the land and bodies of the continent's indigenous. It has a long way to go in order to exorcise that past. It must first want to. The battle over such an exorcism continues. The progress is too damn slow for me.

We drive, walk and otherwise traverse on lands once hunted and farmed by its earliest human inhabitants. It was these people that named the mountains and the rivers, the lakes, the ponds and the creeks. They named their tribes and their elders, their children and their spirits. When the Europeans came they stole the lands, and killed, captured and drove away the people. They even stole the names the slaughtered and hunted had given the places they roamed, and turned them into marketing gimmicks. You know that Pontiac was a leader of a people proud and independent. His name became a brand of automobile with and without fins and bucket seats.

I walk on city streets. I walk on town streets. Every one is desolation row. Those the media call homeless live in almost every situation I encounter. Depending on the benevolence of the municipality they live in, the generosity of the citizens there, the measure of hopelessness these folks live with usually determines their appearance. Having been a few miles down the road of alcohol abuse compounded by poverty, I can appreciate the comfort it provides when tomorrow might be as gloomy as yesterday and the likelihood of a warm bed under a roof is not a thing. The streets were tough when I lived on them in the late 1970s, but for me it was mostly the cops that made them so. Petty harassments, pointless beatings, threats and other forms of assault against the poor, the unkempt and Black people in general seemed to be how police entertained themselves. However, back then it seemed there were enough sisters and brothers of the road to keep one feeling that they were part of something that didn't need to be the end of the road. In addition, the plenty in this so-called land of plenty was not yet mostly hoarded by the richest among us. The selfishness and exploitation that underpins the US economy was under attack by millions who knew there was another way to proceed. This is no longer the case. It certainly seems much harder out there now.

I sometimes wish I was young again—nothing to me except my body, my clothes and the stuff I carried around from town to town, couch to couch. Oh yeah, my heart and soul, too. One to give away to pretty woman who paid me some mind, and the other to keep mostly to myself. I miss the drunken nights when there was always more of the fermented grain to consume. Marijuana was cheap; its availability was subject to the whims of the DEA and various other law enforcement agencies. Sometimes there was none to be found; sometimes it was everywhere and as cheap as Ripple Wine. People lived off of little and nothing. Once I realized I didn't need to spend forty hours or more a week working, I only worked when I needed money for rent, weed or food. That this scenario existed on the scale it did in the 1960s and 1970s but not much longer afterwards seems to prove this lifestyle is unsustainable under capitalism. Our world today provides daily proof of this fact.

Berkeley's People's Park expresses the above in microcosm. Founded in a historical moment of anarchistic joy and street-crazed madness, informed by a revolutionary sense that anything was possible and everything could change, the University of California—who claimed the land the park was created on—has never given up trying to take it back. Its police forces bullied their way onto the land every day harassing and jostling those hanging out

there. The Berkeley City police were usually along for the ride. In other words, it was the cops who have provided most of the edginess, not the folks hanging out there. It was the closest thing I had to an office for a few years in the late 1970s and early 1980s. And the closest thing I wanted to an office, for that matter. Squirrelly dudes selling weed, rough cons in leather and full of malt liquor and wine, pretty hippie women working magic with their smiles, rock and roll music, and acoustic blues. A cast of characters weird enough for any sideshow and real enough to scare off more conventional citizens, while attracting the adventuresome teen, the shore-leave sailor, and the lost children of the American Dream. And the cops. Always the cops.

As I walked onto Telegraph Avenue from Sproul Plaza in 2023, I noticed a few familiar shops were still around. Blondie's Pizza, Rasputin's Records and Moe's Books were among them. Many of the food joints were Asian in nature: Japanese, Chinese, Thai and Korean. There was one very nice almost upscale Cannabis shop.

Despite the continuing assaults on it, People's Park still exists. A backhoe hired by the university to destroy the park in 2022 sat in the middle of the park. Its yellow body was covered with anti-gentrification graffiti, a testament to the ongoing resistance to the development plans the university and certain developers have never stopped attempting. It's reasonable to argue that People's Park was an early response to what would become known as neoliberalism, a form marked by the privatization of public space. The gardens on the west end of the park could use some tending, but they still existed. A hundred or so folks living in tents were spread out in the park's green space. During the three hours I sat in the park eating breakfast and talking with a couple who were sitting nearby, I saw no police. In the past, the police were a constant presence, harassing people for drinking or smoking marijuana. I suppose the legalization of the latter has changed the nature of People's Park, much like it has in many places the herb is no longer an excuse to jail those who imbibe.

After leaving the park I wandered up Telegraph Avenue back to the University. There were only a dozen or so street people hanging out along the Ave. Students rushed by filling the sidewalks. Even here, I only saw a couple cops. When I reached Sproul Plaza, I sat on a bench and watched. There were very few organizations tabling. Those included a table for the Democratic Socialists of America, a couple religious organizations, some frat boys hyping homecoming weekend, and a couple of young men paid to hype nuclear power. While I sat on the bench, there was a test of the emergency warning system. As the siren wailed, hardly anyone seemed to notice. I did notice the student population seems much more diverse in terms of skin tone, ethnicity, and gender fluidity. Watching a trio of young men wearing their ROTC camouflage made me wonder which war they'll be sent to. Students in military uniforms were something I never saw when I lived in Berkeley from 1977-1982. In fact, a guy I knew from that time who never left Berkeley told me it's only been the last fifteen years or so that he's noticed them.[1]

There were these two younger cats who took up residence outside our apartment in Berkeley in 1982. Joe was from Austria and Steve from Sweden. Both were holders of expired student visas. After spending a semester at UC Berkeley, they ran out of money and fell into the lures of the counterculture as it played out on Telegraph Avenue in 1982. Women, weed, song and a pickup truck. That was their life. In July, they built a rather shaky sleeping structure on the pickup and told us they were heading to Colorado. The Grateful Dead were playing there later that month, they needed gas money and we loaded up the pickup. Six humans, sleeping bags, knapsacks, water and several jars of peanut butter, wonder bread and jam. Look out cowboys, here we come. Bob O. joined us at the last minute with a baggie filled with one thousand hits of LSD. With Steve at the helm, the truck headed down Berkeley's University Avenue and on to I-80 East. All was rolling fine until we got to a gas station somewhere east of Reno, Nevada. By then, half the people on the truck were tripping, including Steve. After filling the tank, he wandered off into the desert. The rest of us hung out around the station, talking, eating peanut butter sandwiches and wondering where the hell Steve was. Bob O. mentioned to the owners of the gas station that our driver had wandered off. They laughed. I got their sense of humor. Then they called the Nevada State Police. A cruiser showed up some thirty minutes later. The cops got out of the car, their Smokey the Bear

---

1   As this book was going through the final editing stages, the University of California and the City of Berkeley sent their police into People's Park. Several park users were arrested, their belongings stolen and a fence made of shipping containers double- stacked was erected around the park . The relentless war of capital against the park seems to have won this latest round

hats shading their mirror-shaded faces. The disdain they felt for us was obvious. One of them identified himself as Sgt. — As I watched their faces melt, I explained the situation. They asked everyone for identification. Some complied and they threatened the rest of us, but did nothing else. As we hung around listening to their radios squawk, another cruiser pulled up. The driver lifted his lanky sunburned self out of the front seat, opened the rear door and out stepped Steve. Meanwhile, the Sarge was telling Bob and me that he wasn't going to order an inspection of the vehicle because he didn't want to deal with the paperwork and stink up the closest jail with our smelly flesh. However, he continued, if we stopped anywhere else in Nevada, every trooper was being told to arrest the lot of us. Bob and I told him we would make sure we didn't stop again in his state. Damn right, he responded, unless you want to stay a few years in one of our fine facilities. He wasn't talking about the MGM in Las Vegas.

The trees flashed by my window, their branches green with leaves and the sticky webs of the gypsy moths chewing away entire trees in a day or two. Once when I was hitching from Newburgh, New York to Rochester, Minnesota, I got picked up by a guy whose job was to measure the destruction wrought by these insects in the Adirondacks. The year was 1981. He drove his own pickup truck and kept count of his miles traveled, meals eaten and motel rooms slept in. I rode with him for about half a day in mid-June. We would drive fifty miles on a state road and then go up into the mountains where he took pictures and measurements. I held one end of his tape measure at times. When his day was through, he bought a couple six-packs of Genessee beer which we drank while we sped west to Binghamton, where he let me crash in the bed of his pickup while he rented a motel room. I woke early, found the road west and got picked up in about thirty minutes. That ride took me to a place about fifty miles east of Erie, Pennsylvania. Gypsy moths never die off. It's the summer of 2022 and their larvae are dropping out of trees by the dozens all around New England. One wonders if the unusual heat this summer has something to do with this. Entomology was never my thing, but it's worth investigating. I was a gypsy in 1981 but not a moth. In 2022 I am barely the gypsy I once was. When the journey in 2023 that will define this book begins, I will be back to being that something of that gypsy from my past, albeit a little more wizened and wrinkled.

It was a Vermont afternoon in August of 2022. I was hanging out with some folks who made their home in the woods near Lake Champlain just a bit north of the city, Even though it was too hot for a fire, there was a small one in the camp. I'm guessing it was for cooking cans of soup or whatever. The guy next to me was half asleep. I didn't believe he was high, just tired. The young woman sitting on his other side mentioned he just got off of work, washing dishes down the road. She was around twenty; a slender body and a charming face framed by multicolored hair. Her blue eyes smiled when she talked and she talked a lot. Maybe it was meth that drove her but if it was, she didn't come off like a regular user. Not like the guy on her other side. Nazi tattoos and a wife beater t-shirt stained with sweat. Muscles of sinew and too many prison tattoos to count. He was talking about a one-world government and big pharma. The truth is in the crystal meth he tells me. I ain't buying, and he doesn't care. He rambled on about how only enlightened individuals can defeat the plans already in place. I chuckled, remembering my amphetamine truths when I used to get desoxyn from a friend who robbed pharmacies for narcotics. He sold me one hundred desoxyn for fifty bucks. Those pills kept the short order crew at the pancake house where we worked cooking through twelve hour shifts every Saturday and Sunday for about a year. This guy's crystal use was going to send him back to the can. I laugh, remembering. I don't try to forget.

Swastika leg started talking like the low-rent hustler in Bruce Springsteen's song "Meeting Across the River". He's telling this porcine guy who's been drinking wine for awhile how he's going make a thousand bucks on the morrow. The wine drinker asks on the what, motherfucker? The morrow, dude. What's today, Wednesday? So like tomorrow Thursday. Shakespeare hits the camp of the unhoused, as the poor folks I am sitting with are now called. I stumbled into this camp while walking a trail near the Winooski River a few miles from where it empties into the sixth great lake Lake Champlain. Swastika leg said hey and asked me if I had any money. I told him no and pulled out a joint instead. He didn't want to get high but the rest of the circle did. He's still talking about his hustle. The hustle he wants to pull involves selling some car parts he and a friend stole off the car of some hipster. A catalytic converter and some other stuff. I ask him if he knows the buyer and he says no, man, it's just some cat on Facebook. I tell him it could be a setup and he tells me to shut the fuck up. I get up and leave after giving the girl with the smiling blue eyes and multicolored hair the other joint I had with me. Her mouth smiles and I split, leaving them to their evening. Two weeks later, the young woman with the multicolored hair tells me that the swastika guy is back in prison for violating parole. She laughed while she told me that his big deal was a setup, just like I figured. Talk about walking into a trap. I ran into the girl in a city park. She was cleaned up and somewhat positive about the world. I asked her how it had been going. She told me the cops had turned her over to social services, who in turn hooked her up with a motel room for three months and the possibility of a job. She asked me to go there with her but I begged off and wished her luck. The colors of her hair had faded but her eyes remained the same. There was still a fair amount of hope that showed through. Her friends were discussing whether or not joining the military was a good way to go. One guy, perhaps thirty years old, told them it was the military that fucked him up. When he got back from the Middle East, the army let him go after he left his fort down in Georgia to see his high school girlfriend. That was his story. He was missing three fingers on one hand and claimed he had lost them when emptying trash over in Iraq. Something blew up in his hand. God knows what hidden injuries he had. I asked him if he was getting disability and he said he couldn't because his discharge was dishonorable. Then he said his brother in Georgia was helping him try to get it to at least a general or whatever it takes to get disability. He hoped he didn't have to wait too much longer. I gave him the name and number of a lawyer I knew who helped veterans get their benefits from a bureaucracy all too ready to deny them.

Back on the bus. It was later in 2022. This time it was a Greyhound on its way to Boston. There used to be three or four of these trips every day between Montreal to Boston but COVID checked that schedule. There's only one a day, now. It's usually about two-thirds full. Sometimes you get a seat to yourself and sometimes you don't. The drivers work hard, driving eight to ten hours a day, living out of a backpack and keeping a smile on their face. This one tells his passengers that his name is Elwood, not sir, not Mr. Bus driver, just Elwood, like the Blues Brother in the movies. Elwood is a tall man with wraparound sunglasses and a slight southern accent. The trip itself is all on interstate highways: 89 to 93 to downtown Boston. The scenery in November is suspended somewhere between autumn with its colorful trees and the barrenness of winter in New England. This particular fall there's a lot more green in the fields than in previous ones. The cows lie in the sun watching each other and the traffic, their eyes appearing weary and wise. On occasion, a cellphone comes out and the noise begins. It's somebody's conversation that becomes all of ours. Sometimes it's an angry or excited business person talking numbers and contracts. Sometimes it's a lovers' argument and sometimes it's a kid talking trash. Every episode adds to each participants' drama, if that's what they want. Mercifully, they end, sometimes on their own, and sometimes because the driver demands it. About three hours into the trip we stopped in Hanover, NH with its ivy league feeling. It's almost seventy years since JD Salinger's classic novel of disenchanted modern youth *Catcher in the Rye* was published. Still, every time I'm in this town I think Holden Caulfield is crossing the street to get on the bus. Even though the students at Dartmouth today wear synthetic fibers probably not even invented when JD Salinger penned the book that scandalized the parents of their grandparents when it was published in the 1950s, Hanover reeks of upper class pathos. Not that *Catcher in the Rye* is about Dartmouth, but its preppy upper class setting is what Dartmouth is all about. And the novel could easily be about Dartmouth Prep.

I've mentioned South Station a little before. Crowds of bus goers in one section and train riders in another. The bus section was being renovated. Lots of machinery and people working. The next leg of my journey took me to Portland, Maine. It's a quick and boring ride— more interstate and commuter traffic with trees far to the side of the road when there are any. Occasionally, one catches a glimpse of the Atlantic off to the east. My return journey will be from Rockland, a couple more hours up the coast on US Route One, an old highway built well before the interstate system that actually goes through towns and villages instead of skirting them in the manner of interstates, That ride, while a bit longer, is a pleasant one, in large part because it goes straight into and through a number of towns along its way. Given it is New England, the centers of most of the towns are old and even quaint. It's on the outskirts of these burgs where strip malls line the highway. The stores vary from an occasional stripper bar and stores selling auto parts next to stores selling legal marijuana next to Dollar Stores selling things to the US working class they can no longer afford; things like tools, clothing, kitchen ware and even food. Stuff they used to buy in malls that now sit mostly empty like scenes from a post-apocalypse film out of Hollywood. A Hollywood that produces films that are empty shells of their predecessors. Films about superheroes fulfilling right-wing fantasies of law and order or left-wing fantasies of justice. Truth, justice and the American dollar. The truth is in the pudding, not on the screen. A fellow I'm guessing is in his mid-forties told a woman who let everyone on the bus know she is twenty-one today and on her way to a new job in Augusta, Maine, that if she works hard enough, she'll get the condo she told him she wants. I'm not convinced he believes what he's saying or if his condo dreams have come true, but that myth remains strong. Despite so much evidence against it, people still want to believe they can be okay if they just work their asses off. The awareness for so many that this concept doesn't apply to them is something they refuse to consider until they're living off of 1200 bucks a month of Social Security. Material dreams often become little more than nightmares that put one in the street or a homeless shelter just trying to stay warm.

It's been said many times in many places that the American Dream is alive. The media presents the public with stories of a successful immigrant or an unhoused teen who defies the odds and gets a scholarship to Harvard. These anomalies are presented both as inspiration to the rest of us and, more importantly, serve as deflection; deflection from the facts of life we see on our rides to work and school and deflection from the growing debt we face because our paychecks do not provide enough income to pay for rent, food and utilities. It's impressive how effective this mythology continues to be. I never bought the story, which made it easier for me to ignore the temptations one succumbs to in the pursuit of that so-called dream. Nobody wants to be that person holding a sign asking for work and money. Consequently, most of us will do whatever we can to prevent that from happening to ourselves. That often means putting up with lousy jobs and occasionally abusive bosses. For those without scruples, it can mean a life of petty crime.

The return to Boston began a few days later in the morning. The bus leaves from the ferry terminal in Rockland, Maine. This particular day, fog warnings are posted for pleasure and working boats alike. Lobstermen prepare their materials and vacationers gather their children and belongings. Inside the terminal people drink coffee and buy tickets. The bus comes a little bit before 9:00 AM and we get on, the driver scanning each of our tickets before we board. After traveling through the towns described earlier, we get to Bath, a town built around a giant shipbuilding industry. If it  weren't for Washington's war apparatus, this town would be just one more quaint New England burg. It's the military that keeps it going. The General Dynamics corporation took over the Bath Iron Works in 1995 and is the primary employer in the town. General Dynamics is one of the few companies in the euphemistically labeled defense industry that makes nothing originally intended for the civilian consumer. It's the genuine dealer in death and killing. There's no pretense about making light bulbs or airliners for the private sector. Nothing but blood money. Every manufacturing contract it signs is with the Pentagon. It used to have some of its systems manufacturing based in Burlington, VT. Now, only a few research projects are taking place there. No politician in Vermont liked the occasional protests against the corporation's blood-soaked work, not even Bernie Sanders. This fact alone indicates the mainstream political requirement of support for the US war machine, however hesitant that support might be. General Dynamics' first corporate success seems to have come with its manufacture of the Gatling gun, an early machine gun popularized during the US civil war. In essence, an early weapon of mass destruction. The original Bath shipyard was incorporated in 1884 by a retired Army General named Thomas Hyde. Although the company has made ships for non-military customers, it is the military that keeps it afloat, as it were. People I meet in the area describe the work as dangerous and often repetitive, which often makes it more dangerous. In a region where college is often not considered an option because of its cost, the relatively high pay at the shipyards tempts many a young person. Like other aspects of this part of the Maine coast reminiscent of a half century ago, good-paying blue collar jobs can still be found at the shipyard. One contemporary negative for potential workers are the random drug tests done on employees due to the corporation's many contracts with the Pentagon. Marijuana is legal for adults in Maine but federal regulations override local laws in these kinds of scenarios.

The first several miles of the journey to Boston, the bus cruises down a pleasant country road running parallel to the coast but inland to where the ocean is not visible. There are fewer than a dozen passengers, all of whom are quietly engaged. Some Hollywood movie that involves explosions and boats is playing on the video screens that hang above certain seats. Nobody is watching. Double wide trailers share the land on both sides of the road with farmhouses of varying size. Most appear to be one hundred years old at least; wooden clapboards peeling paint serve as siding on about half, while vinyl siding covers the rest. Propane tanks and woodpiles are the preferred sources of fuel. Occasionally, I see a house with its four sides covered by cedar shingles, reminding me of a summer on Cape Cod spent shingling a cottage under the direction of my kid's grandfather.

The occasional campaign sign supporting one or the other candidate disrupts the quiet landscape. Like much of the nation in 2022, Maine has two very distinct choices in the race for governor. One is the extreme right-wing candidate, Paul Lepage, a proto-fascist masquerading as a libertarian. The other is a classic liberal and current governor named Janet Mills. Her rhetoric focuses on affordable health care, keeping marijuana legal, and maintaining the right to reproductive freedom. Lepage was governor when Maine voters passed a referendum legalizing weed and setting up retail shops to sell it. Lepage ignored the new law and refused to allow the  shops to open. He also opposed the expansion of Medicaid to help people afford medical care. Many of those who voted for him previously were the same folks negatively affected by his decisions regarding both. (He lost the election).

The town of Damariscotta is a typical coastal Maine town. US Route One serves as its Main Street, just as it does for many towns along the east coast. Small shops crowd along it, old brick and wood buildings with signs declaring the tenant's business. The morning sun reflecting off the inlet to the east, its silver glow highlighting the buildings. It's scenes like this that suggest why American artists from the region developed their illuminated style — from Edward Hopper's painting done during his summers on the Maine coast, to the living artist Paul Batch.

Some of the first commercial enterprises one sees getting off I-95 going into Boston are ones selling cars. Then come at least three Italian restaurants, all of them advertising pasta and cocktails. The strip malls go from ones with new facades to ones that look much the same as they did in the 1980s when they were built. The road, which runs from Revere into east Boston, is reminiscent of Route One between Baltimore and Washington; a mishmash of commercial, industrial and residential properties, all a bit worn-looking but apparently still functional. One almost expects to see a Ford Fairlane or maybe even a Pontiac Barracuda busting its pipes down the road in a blaze of asphalt glory from a mid-1970s Bruce Springsteen song. Or, more appropriately, I suppose, would be a Jonathan Richman song about suburban Boston and a shopping mall. After navigating the one-way streets of downtown Boston, the bus arrives at South Station. We disembark. It's the end of this particular line.

My son and his family were outside the station. We headed to Providence. It's a straight shot down the highway. My grandson filled me in on his life from the back seat. Bob Marley music was playing most of the ride. He's my grandson's favorite. We spent the next couple days going to the beach, playing games in the yard, walking around Providence and talking on their deck, often with a tasty brew in hand. A few days later, I took a commuter train back to South Station. I was heading back to Vermont.

While I waited for my bus ride from South Station to Burling-

44

ton, a woman dressed in a baseball hat, jeans and a Jimi Hendrix t-shirt began talking to me. Her short, curly hair stuck out from under her hat. "Who sang the song that goes, 'Hello darkness, my old friend…?'" "Simon and Garfunkel." I replied. She told me I looked like a person who would know and then wondered if I liked chocolate donuts. Not especially was my reply, but I do like jelly-filled. "I ain't got none of those." She said as she reached into her pocket and pulled out a paper bag which held a chocolate donut. We started talking about Bill Wilson and Alcoholics Anonymous; she reminded me that Wilson was the founder. Then she told me about a place she visited in Vermont when she was in rehab for alcohol issues. Her bus was announced just as she finished describing the sleeping quarters there. As she walked away, she sang Praise Be over and over. I watched as she boarded the Greyhound to New York City and overheard the driver telling her she needed to be quiet on the bus. She nodded her head in assent. For some reason, she reminded me of a woman a friend and I met when we rode from Oakland, CA to Atlanta, Georgia in 1979. Our supplies for the trip included three packs of Players cigarettes, a couple of pints of vodka, some blotter acid, and a dozen pre-rolled joints of half-assed weed we would smoke at each rest stop. I'm not sure why we bothered. It rarely did anything but make us cough.

The bus stations themselves left a lot to be desired back then. This was well before the panopticon public spaces we live in today where all is surveilled, recorded and transmitted to the authorities. Most stations were policed by a combination of rent-a-cops and local police up until the 2000s, with special attention often paid to the bathrooms where procurers, pimps and others in the sleazier end of the sex trade would work. Cops actually went undercover in the DC Greyhound terminal in 1970s hoping to bust a ring of procurers looking for teenage runaways of all genders. I suppose they were successful and can only imagine the damage that kind of work did do their souls. New York's Port Authority had its own set of cops who lurked in the terminal trying to keep an eye on the madness there.

Although the hubbub of a big city bus terminal will probably never change, nowadays the cops and other law enforcement types are too numerous to count. In some cities they are also menacingly armed in outfits straight out of a dystopian sci-fi film. I was in Manhattan on September 11, 2001. When I went to the bus terminal in midtown the day after the towers fell, it was surrounded by military types in full uniform carrying lots of weaponry and wearing armor. A disheveled human lay on the sidewalk just outside the doors near Madison Square Garden. While I talked with the cops about when they thought the terminal might re-open, I noticed a smell like death. It was coming from that person. After the cop told me he figured it would be another couple days before the buses were running again, I mentioned that the person laying on the sidewalk had been there for a few hours and might need some help. He radioed for an ambulance. I waited around to see what would happen. After checking the person's pulse and other signs, the officer was informed that the man was dead. I had to answer a couple questions before I headed back to my friend's (whom I'll call Antigone) apartment. That was not the last time a bus terminal in the US looked like a military base.

In November 2001, I took a Greyhound from Burlington, Vermont to New York City to attend a Bob Dylan concert at the Garden. While passengers waited in the parking lot of the Burlington bus terminal a couple of young, muscular men in blue windbreakers began approaching people in the crowd and asking them for identification. Most people who weren't asked ignored the two. I was curious as to what agency they were working for. I noticed they were only asking people whose skin was not white for ID. Given that it was barely two months since September 11th, I assumed this was part of the new security apparatus being put in place by the George W. Bush regime. Sure enough, when one of the men asked a Haitian woman near me for her identification I saw the logo for the Immigration and Naturalization Service (INS, now part of Homeland Security) on his jacket. I asked him why he was checking identification, mostly just to see what he would say. At first he ignored me, and then he told me it was none of my concern if I was a US citizen. I answered that the fact that I was a US citizen did make it my business. He looked at me with a look that mixed annoyance with something approaching contempt. Then his cohort came over and told him they had checked everyone "that needed to be checked." As they got in their US Government vehicle, I wondered how intense the security apparatus would end up becoming. I continue to ride Greyhound buses between Vermont and various northeastern cities. Riders are now required to show identification when they purchase a ticket and drivers are instructed to ask for ID when passengers board. In the terminals, law enforcement is often joined by military types with automatic weapons. It's just the way it is. The Bob Dylan show was great. He sang his New York songs with an added emotion. I'm guessing it was because of the events earlier that year on September 11th. My friend Antigone, who had never seen Dylan before, took me to a bar near the Garden afterwards to meet some of her friends. The bar was full of firefighters and off-duty cops. We had a good time playing darts.

This book began to take shape in the summer months of 2022. The absurdity of some kind of a war with Russia was looming. More surprising than that, there were people that seemed to be looking forward to such a thing. Had COVID really put them in a place where a vicious and bloody cataclysm between two self-centered and militarized nations was a reasonable way to resolve what author Ishmael Reed correctly labeled another European tribal war? Was the population of the United States having a grand flashback influenced by the lack of imagination amongst the current crop of bought-off and pathetic politicians? Had the madness finally reached a place where bringing down the planetary temple was a reasonable consideration? Or were the merchants of death just short on profits? I mean, what the fuck was wrong with these people? The fact that the main congressional opposition to funding and thereby escalating this war had so far come from the libertarian wing of the Republican party was both unsurprising and uncomfortable. The history between Washington and post-Soviet Kyiv—a history that presents a clear timeline regarding the increasing involvement of Washington in Ukrainian politics — has been mostly erased from US mainstream media outlets and replaced with an absurd version of history peppered with outright lies. My cynical self remembers the words of R. Crumb's character Mr. Natural, sitting on a tractor and saying "'Twas ever thus..." And I suppose it was.

I guess when I was younger and a little less jaded my perspective was different; I believed there was some hope in this system that wants to rule. I don't remember ever being completely sold on the American myth, though. Especially after I discovered there were separate drinking fountains for white and Black people when our family moved to Maryland in 1959. I was five almost six. My father told me the reason as neutrally as possible. However, being from Minnesota where America's racial apartheid was economic but not legal, he wasn't used to separate facilities based on race. Nor did he feel right about defending them.

There's something rotten in the United States, something that has festered for a long time, but was allowed and even encouraged to grow exponentially since this century began. We've all watched it grow and now even those who once believed it could be fought, and therefore fought it, are beginning to question the point of doing so. It seems that no matter what one does to challenge the status quo, things continue their downward trend. The tsunami of war, racism, inequality accentuated by climate disaster — all of which are fostered by capitalism and an intensified greed among those with the most has yet to crest. Or so it seems. Nothing is immune. The wealthy have their hands in everything from rock and roll to religion, kindergarten to college, gasoline to granola; the only defining characteristic that matters is how the hell can profit be extracted?

How the hell can they grab it all? Like hoarders on steroids, their piles of cash and bitcoin climb to incomprehensible numbers. The devil's on the loose. His accomplices and his tools are in the banks and the pool halls, Congress, and the White House. Every single fucking corporation on the Dow Jones. Most of the churches and pretty much everyone walking around in uniforms with leaves and stars on their shoulders in the Pentagon and every goddamn joint military base. Nobody could die for their sins and make a difference. Hell, everybody could die for their sins and it wouldn't. Then, again, we all may. Sure, there's folks selling Jesus but it sure doesn't sound like the guy written about in the gospels. That Jesus might have risen from the dead to save us from our sins, but even his image is being bought and sold in the name of the dollar bill. I've got to admit I feel sorry for the believers who think their false prophet is the real thing — not that I know or truly care what the real thing is — but I can sure as hell tell a fake when I see one, and there's fake prophets everywhere. It's a bit of a trope by now, but most believers wouldn't even know the real Jesus if he knocked on their door or asked them for a dollar on the street. Instead, they might even shoot him.

Left my home in Burlington, VT. heading for Sacramento, CA… …I'm trying for a personal version of Chuck Berry's song "The Promised Land". Even though I can fit the meter of the tune in if I strum my guitar just right, the version I'm attempting doesn't have the same zing, the same ring like the one Mr. Berry or any of those rockers who followed in his footsteps had with the tune. Then again, I'm not any kind of Johnny B. Goode. I play a little guitar, but I don't ring any bells. Plus, there's to be no ground transportation on this leg of the trip. No Greyhound, no passenger train, just a jet airliner or two across the great prairie, the amber waves of grain and the cities below.. Plane trips just don't have the same romance as trains, buses, and automobiles tend to have. If hitchhiking was still anything but the death wish it seems to be now, I might have kept it in my repertoire. I believe those days are long gone. One of the greatest hitchhiking songs—Me and Bobby McGee—is just a song about the past now, and the highways are now less free. Indeed, several are now toll roads especially designed for working professionals so they can get to work as fast as possible without hanging in the six lane traffic jams with the rest of the working folks. There's one stretch of such road in Virginia that changes its pricing depending on traffic flow, time of day and so on. I've seen the cost go up to forty dollars for one passage. Monopoly capitalists call it dynamic pricing. It's used to sell parking spots in certain cities, concert and sporting events tickets and who knows what else. The capitalists attribute this practice to supply and demand. The rest of us call it price gouging and attribute it to the greed of the corporate masters.

Airports are some of the most modern of architectures. Oppressive buildings with lots of things to buy. There are no windows that open to the outside; most doors contain locks only certain employees can open and the lights are never completely darkened. Public address announcements repeat their warnings about flights that are boarding and reminding everyone to stay close to their luggage. It's a security measure that may or may not make sense. Essentially, they are minimum security prisons we pay to enter, albeit only for a few hours at a time. There are gates to keep you in or keep you out, and cops every few hundred feet, with Starbucks almost as ubiquitous. Cameras surreptitiously (and not so surreptitiously) placed record every action their eyes can see, which is almost every action in the area inside and out. Bars, restaurants and taverns offer a pretense of choice usually at a higher price than on the outside. Pretty lights and shiny things sit behind the storefront glass, all credit cards accepted. The USA in a microcosm. Lots of people in a hurry to get in line and wait for things out of their control. That latter fact causes those used to being in control a fair amount of consternation, which a few take out on the clerks standing behind their counters trying to keep that trademark smile on their face. One can imagine the things workers talk about when and if they get a break. I know what I would be saying about the customers who really acted like they needed a slap across the face. I traveled via plane during the COVID lockdown

51

only because my father was dying. The only thing positive I can say about the experience was that I could buy a beer in one part of the airport and take it to another. Before and since the lockdown, most airports require one to drink the beverage in the food court it was purchased at. Other than that, flying was just more stressful than traveling should be. People were not necessarily kinder, people who were obnoxious before were still obnoxious, and the security forces were about the same. In other words, never invisible and often overly aggressive. I truly felt bad for the workers who staffed the restaurants, airline desks and provided services to passengers. Their jobs appeared to be even more unlikable. It's a long way from those flights as a kid in the 1960s when they served steak and eggs for breakfast and even gave the coach class passengers a choice of meals. Or those in the 1970s when the alcohol flowed like water and the flight attendants had time to be kind.

Ever since the cell phone became ubiquitous, there are always people talking business on their phones in airports and other transportation hubs, as if it's the most important thing in the world. Then again, I suppose it is for most of those conducting it. I've heard numbers being thrown back and forth and discussions about upcoming interviews and employees being let go. The casual nature of it all used to startle me, but that was a couple decades ago when cell phones began to appear in the hands of businessmen and women.. Still the banality of it all throws me. The artificial light and the nervous hubbub in airports reminds me of a casino. Of course, in the Las Vegas airport terminals *are* casinos.

The first time I rode public transportation was when my grandmother took my brother and me on a streetcar in downtown Minneapolis. We were on our way to see a Christmas movie and eat pancakes afterwards. I was eight years old. When our family moved to Frankfurt am Main in Germany, I began riding public transit daily. The system was complex and included streetcars, subways, buses and trains between cities. Travel around the city and its suburbs was cheap — maybe ten cents a ride — and it increased my independence a hundredfold. Ever since, public transit has been my primary form of transportation. Consequently, I am always surprised when I talk with people who have never ridden it once. Not even a Greyhound bus to another city or town. The effectiveness of the automobile industry in convincing cities and towns to close down their trolleys, streetcars and even bus systems after World War Two and replace them with wide roads and interstate highways is something to behold. Even more, the fact that its advertising convinced the vast majority of US residents that driving a car is the best way to get around is an even more impressive feat of advertising than that which addicted millions of people to cigarettes. Most people are surprised when I tell them I have never had a driver's license and have only driven about eighty miles my entire life. It was on a stretch of I-10 in the Arizona desert west of Phoenix. The guy who picked me up was a fugitive from something — the law, a marriage, the military — he never said. He did give me a couple hits of speed (white crosses if I recall) as soon as I got in his car and talked about his journey from somewhere in Mississippi. I sort of listened as the crosses took effect. Around two in the morning he pulled over to the side of the highway and asked me to drive. I told him I had never driven. After his initial surprise, he told me it was no big deal, then told me I just needed to stay on the road; an easy task on this stretch of I-10. Flat, straight and no trees or even cacti to run into should the vehicle stray off the asphalt. I took the wheel, he went to sleep, and I drove about forty miles in an hour until he woke up, whereupon he resumed driving. The adrenaline intensified the speed in my veins. My heart was still racing when the sun began rising behind us. The colors of the desert sunrise glowed shades of red and yellow.

53

I read a statistic somewhere that in 1920 the network of interurban trolley system was so dense that a determined rider could take an electric trolley from Waterville, Maine to Sheboygan, Wisconsin. I can't vouch for the veracity of that claim, but I do remember a friend in Olympia, Washington who figured out a way to take city buses from Olympia to Seattle. This was in the 1980s, when public transit in the Pacific Northwest was poorly administered and assumedly poorly funded. The trip took a while, but only cost three or four dollars. It was a scenic route, taking the rider through downtowns and strip malls, industrial districts, and parklands. There were periods where one waited up to an hour for the next connection and sometimes the bus didn't come, doubling or even tripling the wait time at stops that were occasionally in rather sketchy neighborhoods.

A similar situation exists now in most of Vermont. If one is patient, one can ride a series of public transit buses from Burlington to spots two and three hours away. The cost for such trips is small. However, in much of the United States, there are entire counties with no public transit and, in some cases, no private carriers, either. Many of them used to have the privately owned carriers Greyhound and Trailways coming through two or three times a day. It's almost like the elimination of any kind of public transit was planned. Even if it wasn't, it's the fact that in the US public transportation must make a profit that has helped lead to its demise. One of neoliberal capital's primary enemies is public ownership of anything, from transit to energy to schools.

The first time I remember hearing the classic American song "Goin' Down the Road Feelin' Bad" was in junior high. One of the teachers had a Woody Guthrie record and played a couple tunes from it while he taught us about the Great Depression. "Do Re Mi" is the one I recall. He lent me the album one weekend. I discovered the tune. Then I don't remember hearing it again until I heard it a couple of years later on a Grateful Dead live recording. I've never gone down a road feeling bad, though. Hungry, thirsty and dirty, but never bad. The road was my salvation when the world I found myself in was stagnant and sour, filled with hassles and boredom. Being on the road is a freedom of a certain kind. Cars going by and leaving me in their dust. Cars going by then pulling over to give me a lift. It's all a part of the traveling game. It's a game I was born into and still can't get enough of. Hey, Neal Cassady.

As I said earlier, if hitchhiking were still a reasonable possibility, I might have used my thumb for some of the wandering I did while writing this book. But it isn't. Nobody feels safe anymore; not the drivers or the hitchhikers. In recent years I've hitched a couple miles around the town I live in, but my last major hitchhiking journey was in 1982. I went from Berkeley, California to Austin, Texas. From there I wandered around the Midwest with no particular place to go. The rides didn't seem any harder to get than in the previous couple of years, but they tended to be shorter distance. That meant a lot of standing on the side of the road in a number of different locales. One ride took me from Austin to a service station in the emptiness that defines so much of Texas. I fell asleep on the side of the road after drinking a few Lone Stars. When I awoke, an Apache woman lay next to me in her own sleeping bag. We drank some coffee I bought at the service station and caught a ride up the road. A couple hours later, our ride dropped us off. She went in one direction and I went in another. The next ride was in a van driven by two fellows on their way to a biker gathering at some artificial lake near Dallas. The two men were wired on crystal. I took a line when they offered. When we reached the destination I hung out and listened to the country blues band playing there, grabbed some ribs and a couple beers, ate and split before the gathering took an edge I was familiar with from previous biker gatherings. The speed kept me awake through the night and well into the next day. By then I was in a Toyota traveling towards Oklahoma City. The driver was a GI on leave going to visit his brother in a state prison near Oklahoma City. He let me out about ten miles from the entrance. This presented a problem. I had seen several signs telling drivers not to pick up hitchhikers because they might be escapees from the prison. I did eventually get a ride from a carload of Grateful Dead fans going to the band's concert at the Oklahoma City Zoo. Being a fan myself, it couldn't have worked out much better. I was going down the road, but I wasn't feeling bad. In fact, it was almost like I was going to where the water tasted like wine. I was that like that diving duck in the song about the river of whiskey. I was swimming to the bottom and I was going to drink my way up. And not care if I didn't.

Part of me feels like I'm cheating. No thumb stuck out on the side of the road. No stories from drivers telling me how Jesus can save me from myself and the mean old world, or that what I really should do is join the army — it will give me the discipline I need for a successful life. No dude trying to convince me a blowjob is just a blowjob, so let's pull into this rest stop up ahead. No smelly guy sitting in a hobo jungle sharpening his hunting knife telling those of us just drinking and staying warm why he had to kill someone, but I'm not really listening because I don't want to really know, even if his story is all bullshit. No nervous sweat when a cop car stops and the uniformed driver starts walking towards me, his hand unsnapping his holster and then resting on the gun there; my mind trying to remember if I have any contraband somewhere on my person. Also thinking to myself, trying to measure up if this is the cop that's going to let loose and beat the shit out of me because he can. I don't miss those negatives at all.

Yeah, part of me feels like I'm cheating. Then again, I'm just riding coach. No private bathroom or cabin with a bed and sheets.

It's the less than a hundred dollar ticket from Sacramento to Portland, Oregon. No frills. Not even Wi-fi. And I'm good with that. One can only experience the pure wondrousness of the American landscape by placing oneself in places throughout this vast continent, after all. There remains a beauty in this land that has not been destroyed by the pursuit of profit or the arrogance of man. Not yet, anyhow. Even in this nation's less desirable places, that beauty can be found. If you look at it right.

I was waiting for the train at the depot in Essex, Vermont. The conversation began like many others between strangers in the USA. A man was pacing back and forth in the very small depot. He wore a baseball hat that said Army. Sports is almost always an icebreaker. He and his wife were heading to Philadelphia for the 2022 Army-Navy game. Money had, as it does so often in sports, made the game too big for the football field at either academy. Now it was played in big NFL stadiums. From the banter about the game, the conversation turned to the military itself. Turned out that the couple both came from so-called military families: several members in the Navy and a couple in the Army. Lots of time spent in uniforms. Too much time spent in wars. I understood in my own way. My dad spent thirty years in the Air Force. We traveled often. My memories of the travel and the increased awareness it created are fond, but I'm not convinced all my siblings share the sentiment.

The war and military side of dad's career were just something I put up with while we spent our years in places like Pakistan where the days were always warm, the mountains high and the Pakistanis we met and knew widened my understanding of humanity. Or our years in Germany's cities living lives considerably more free and certainly more interesting than those we might have spent in suburbia. Those wars, though. I just wonder at the arrogance of those who think they can rule the world or that they should.

I was going to Maryland again. It was a few weeks before the 2022 winter holidays — Christmas, if you like. It seemed like a good time to visit my siblings. I got to the station at BWI Airport around 9:30 in the evening. My older sister picked me up and we drove to her house about twenty minutes away. The train ride had been uneventful. Although it was crowded from Springfield, Massachusetts to Manhattan, I had two seats to myself from Penn Station all the way to my destination. The weather was sunny and the temperature above freezing. I watched shorebirds and a couple herons fish and scavenge in the wetlands in northern New Jersey. There's a section of Jersey somewhere around Newark where the waste of the metropolis is filtered though marshlands. The reeds and cattails grow high, the oil floats on parts of the watery surface, its rainbow of colors shifting in paisley designs. Majestic herons and other shorebirds reside in these wetlands, eating frogs and who knows what else. Every time the train passes through those environs, I can't help marvel at nature's ability to neutralize the work of humanity. As dusk slipped into darkness, the conversation on the train diminished. I quietly drank a beer. Some passengers grabbed a quick nap while others watched films on their laptops. Most of the remaining passengers in my car departed in Philadelphia.

It was Christmas time in the city. I went to a German style Christmas market in downtown Baltimore with a couple of sisters and a brother-in-law. We drank Hofbrau beer on tap and ate wurst and brotchen. The weather was sunny and warmer than usual for December. The next day we went walking through a wealthy part of Alexandria, Virginia known as Old Town. I saw wreaths on most of the doors, an extraordinary number of luxury vehicles in the narrow streets and caught glimpses of the world cup on TV in bars we walked past. The contrast between the wealth of Old Town and the working class environment of Baltimore was impossible to ignore.

There's a website run by the U.S. Army detailing its long and bloody history. The language used on the site reflects West Point's continued belief that its graduates and their subordinates are forces of good, perhaps even divinely employed. The histories of the so-called Indian wars on the site — wars that were essentially genocidal campaigns of murder, rape and destruction — are couched in language that considers each battle, each war to be necessary for what Washington called and calls "continued expansion". The history on the site is an appalling read, but important if one really wants to know how the powerful truly think. And what the actual history of this nation truly is. To its credit, the US Army doesn't sugarcoat the facts. There's no pretending that the intention was anything other than the theft of land, the destruction of people's lives and environment, and the eventual occupation of those lands so that more destruction could occur without military opposition. Author Richard Drinnon called it "the politics of Indian-hating" in his book that included the phrase in its title. On its website, the US Army leaves the emotion out of the equation and just calls it killing.

The plane from Burlington arrived in Chicago's O'Hare airport with time to spare. My belly told me to find a beer and a burger. A restaurant called Chili's appeared, and I sat at the bar. An attractive Latina woman poured me an IPA and put in the order for a burger. She told me later she was from Puerto Rico. Her family moved to Chicago after hurricane Maria destroyed much of the island. The irony, she tells me, is that her parents were the first in two generations to actually live on the island. Her great grandparents had moved to Chicago for work back in the 1950s. Or so she thought. She brought me another IPA. A big man who had been sitting in front of me on the plane sat down next to me. He removed his Chevy hat with a USA flag superimposed over the Chevy logo. We talked about his plans to drive his Harley from San Diego all the way up the Pacific Coast Highway in the summer of 2023. He remarked, "It'll be just like the time I did it in 1971 after the Army let me go — except now I'm old and chunky. And I got no hair." I smiled and drank my beer.

I was heading right back where I started from. California here I come. Sacramento's lights appeared beyond the airliner's wing, growing ever denser the closer to the airport we get. The landing was about as graceful as a big jetliner landing can be. My brother Tim was waiting at the curb when I left the airport terminal. After a quick hug we hit the road. The ride to Folsom was less than an hour. I said hi to his wife, Mary Beth, and we sat down for a wind-down brew before bed. I was operating on east coast time and was fuckin' tired. The next day was already here. As it turned out, that one beer became three.

The next day, after a leisurely morning of breakfast and a walk to a nearby dam and reservoir along a trail named after Johnny Cash, we headed to Sam Horn's, a small pub my brother favors. In fact, he has a tab there. As always, the conversation was lively and the beer selection more than adequate. Located on a street in what the town calls Folsom's historic district, the street had begun over a century earlier as a small trading post for gold rush dreamers and the scammers, gunslingers and others looking to profit from the pursuit of the riches that shiny metal represents to the world. The greed,

rapaciousness, racism and violence glorified in the history of the gold rush is representative of US history. Those tales include plenty of booze, clever card sharks, slick women, their equally slick male companions and those they trafficked, and greed. That, and very little shame. No shame for the trafficked women, the shootings over gold and card games, the destruction of the lands and the people living there. Rough, raw and rowdy capitalism cannot afford shame. It only gets in the way of profit and allows those with consciences into the conversation, be they preachers or union organizers, Pride and arrogance are the natural allies of the true American capitalist; that man or woman whose primary goal is the top place in the yearly Fortune 500. Shame, like other phenomena calling on a human's better nature, gets in the way of avarice, while avarice is the perfect foundation for the pursuit of profit.

The conversations during this drinking session ranged from the music of Pink Floyd and String Cheese Incident to the politics of libertarianism and the untidiness of capitalism. Those last two topics always provoke some excited exchanges between my brother's co-workers and me. Despite our fundamental differences about the benefits of capitalism (I'm not convinced it really has any when it comes to the greater good), the conversations always seem to find certain surprising points of agreement. The beverages add their own element, loosening our tongues and ensuring a fair amount of laughter.

The other historical focal point of the town of Folsom besides Old Town is the state prison. Made famous, more or less, via the Johnny Cash song "Folsom Prison Blues," the facility occupies many acres of land. My brother likes to say it has the best remaining undeveloped acreage around. I believe he has a point, although the land just outside its numerous walls and fences is similar. The landscape is a uniquely California one. The closest thing to it I've ever seen was in parts of Italy where olive groves dominate. Manzanita trees wind their trunks around themselves, small creeks and rivers run through the patches of vegetation. Of course, the creeks grow smaller as the weather dries up, their trickles slowly making their way to the American River, the river where the indigenous Nisenan coexisted with the land the river ran through. In 1833, almost seventy-five percent of the tribe died in a malaria epidemic. Then came the discovery of gold. The *California Historical Society Quarterly* describes what happened: "During the summer of 1849 a small detachment of troops had been sent to Johnson's Rancho, on the Bear River, to establish a post for the purpose of preventing conflicts between the Indians and the increasing number of settlers at the mines of the Yuba and Feather rivers ... for the purpose of putting an end to outrages that were then being committed by the whites upon the Indians of that neighborhood." Then the government in Washington, DC took the land away from the tribes under the auspices of the Barbour Treaties. It never gave them any of the land the natives were promised — not even on a reservation. These treaties were signed in secret and were never ratified by Congress. This context makes it clear they were never meant to mean a damn thing. Subsequent history proves that. One more set of lies. Indigenous people have heard them all. They continue to be ignored by most of the people living in the lands their ancestors once roamed. Meanwhile, they rank first in many categories that define poverty.

The Johnny Cash Trail runs for several miles along the border of the prison grounds. Paved and about ten feet wide, it is used by walkers and bike riders. My brother explained that the trail was supposed to be more of a memorial to Cash than it actually is, but the fundraising seemed to disappear into god knows where. I asked if he thought someone was pocketing the funds for their own use, but he refused to speculate, saying that he didn't know enough about it to comment. However, he did have his suspicions. Several camps of

the unhoused are hidden away in the manzanita stands along the creek beds. When it comes to places to live outside, one could do worse than those camps. As occurs in most places around the US, the police occasionally shut down the camps, big and small. This happens more often in the summer when the fear of fire is greatest, a legitimate fear, as the last several years have shown. The more the area gets developed, the greater the chance people's residences will burn, if for no other reason than that there are more buildings. Also like other places everywhere in the United States, the services available to the unhoused in the county varies according to the whims of the local governments and the abilities of non-profits to spread their funds out in a manner that helps most.

Somehow, we have adjusted to this reminder of how the US economic system works. The unhoused are a fact of life in cities and towns, big and small. Their lives are lived out in our streets, shopping areas, churches and schools. I don't believe most people believe that the houseless deserve their lot. At the same time, it seems too many are looking for a reason to escape the harsh truth they represent. The stark reality of the unhoused's presence is a constant reminder how tenuous a life dependent on the current version of capitalism actually is. The understanding that there but for the grace of a few thousand or a few hundred dollars go you or I has not been so true in the United States in perhaps a hundred years

Tim, his wife Mary Beth, and I discussed this on and off during my visit. Our income levels are quite different. We have taken different paths through our lives and arrived where we are in part because of that. Yet, compassion is not specific to class, skin tone, or gender. It is part of the human species' DNA, despite the greedy among us who pretend otherwise. We all agreed the crisis of the unhoused is a crisis of capitalism. More specifically, it is a crisis resulting from the mutation of the dream of home ownership into a nightmare investment. Hardly anyone buys a house thinking they will remain in it until they die. More likely, it is bought as an investment that increases in value like a stock portfolio is supposed to. The fact that the US economic system encourages, nay demands, that one be ready to forsake their home to turn a profit is an all too real scenario for many US homeowners. Each ripple in the economy created by this manipulation of what is unabashedly called "the housing market" sends more folks into the associated scams of high rents and facilities for the poor. The constant increase in housing prices means more and more working people cannot afford to buy a home; sometimes it means they can't afford to pay rent, either. Without the ability to purchase a house, those without good credit and an ability to procure a down payment are left to the often cruel whims of the rental market. As we all know, this group of people is mostly made up of people who work their asses off and, in the terms set forth regarding the so-called work ethic, deserve a home they know they won't be evicted from.

Along with visits to brewpubs,, watching concert recordings of Bruce Springsteen on television, listening to plenty of music and conversations ranging from religion to Trump, Grateful Dead to Bill Monroe and David Crosby (who died while I was there), the price of eggs and the cooking of sourdough, we picked dozens of oranges fruiting on the trees in their yard. California is like that, even when it's wet and chilly. Every time I visit I wonder how I can get back sooner rather than later. I took a few of the oranges with me. My friends in Portland would appreciate them.

Four days after my arrival in California, it was time to catch my train to Portland, Oregon. I arrived at the train station in Sacramento around 11:00 PM for an 11:49 departure. The station smelled like someone's dirty laundry. The train arrived on time.

There was a bit of confusion among the passengers but the conductors were kind and helpful. All aboard! After finding a seat, I couldn't help overhearing a young hippie woman trying to control what sounded like a confused relationship off the train from her seat and phone on the train. A youngster began to whine. The train was on the move. We rumbled slowly out of the station. Mama told the toddler it was going to be okay, but the kid didn't sound like he was buying it.

The train was called the Coast Starlight. The night went by and the train rolled on. The lights of Sacramento reflected in the river before they disappeared in the darkness. The Albion coast was to our left. Its history included hippie communes and shipwrecked sailors. In fact, there were so many communes on the Albion coast in the late 1960s and 1970s, the communards established a network among themselves. Known as the Albion Nation, it was rivaled only by a similar network of communes in Vermont known as Free Vermont. The Free Vermont collaborators tended to be more politically oriented, most likely because of the larger percentage of new left radicals who were involved. The departure of the train resolved the hippie woman's issues as the tracks took her north, presumably leaving her troubles behind. As the night rolled on, a woman cussing up a storm on her phone stopped after a conductor asked her to, while an older man snored like he was in a king-sized bed in a soundproof room. Fortunately, he stopped snoring when the train halted to let a freight train pass by. Overall, the night passed uneventfully; I slept for an hour or two here and there, accumulating my rest during the course of the night.

The unusual rains this winter had turned the landscape on the eastern side of the coastal California ranges into a verdant carpet of valleys and rolling hills; sheep, cattle and trucks dotted the fields, lending their presence to a breathtaking scene. After

ultimately putting together a fairly decent night's sleep, I awoke to a sunrise somewhere in northern California. A few clouds, and a dusting of snow on the hills tinged with red and lined in gold. A few other early risers shared the view, drinking coffee and eating microwave breakfast sandwiches. Some farm vehicles drove by on the road parallel to the track. The sun rose over the hills — pinks, oranges and golden hues lending a beauty straight out of an impressionist painter's palette. It was quiet and it was beautiful. The wheels clicked and clacked underneath.

When we crossed the border into Oregon, the trees got denser and taller. Of course, this meant that Paul Bunyan's successors would be working. The timber industry may have shrunk since the first time I was in the Pacific Northwest in 1985, but it was far from dead. Sure enough, in the Oregon woods near Churmult I began to see logging trucks rolling down the road. I couldn't help thinking that if humans were as smart as they think they are, they would back away from the profit-determines-everything philosophy that has been wreaking havoc of all kinds on the earth and its inhabitants. It's a thought I have all too often, with good reason. I know I'm not the only one thinking it, either. Activities like logging old growth timber convinces me that humans are not as smart as they think they are.

My friend Stephanie was picking me up at Portland's Union Station. As the train made its way slowly toward the downtown station, it rolled through industrial sections of Portland and along the Williamette river. We crossed an older bridge — one of many in Portland. The conductors walked through the train calling out the stop and reminding disembarking passengers to make certain they took all of their belongings with them when they departed. As we rolled through downtown, I was slightly surprised at the small numbers of homeless encampments and their relatively small size. The last time I had been in Portland about six years previous, the camps were numerous and often housed hundreds of folks left without a home in the rapidly gentrifying city. Although I liked to think the decrease in the numbers of the unhoused was related to public and non-profit agencies helping them to get off the streets, I knew that police violence and raids of encampments were the more likely cause. The proof was partially present in the greater number of newly-built tall buildings downtown — most likely housing offices, many of which were empty after the COVID lockdowns. The optimism of the high tech bros and their virtual inventions designed to produce quick wealth and often not much else was not a match for the unleashed virus. San Francisco would end up suffering a similar fate on an even greater scale as the financial fallout from the pandemic took its toll. There was a lot more graffiti on the bridges and sides of warehouses, empty storefronts and other canvases, much of it anti-police. ACAB (All

Cops are Bastards) was a favorite; obviously a testimony to the anti-police brutality protests that the Portland police and their fascist friends turned into battlegrounds in 2020 following the police murder of George Floyd in Minneapolis. There were also some pretty spectacular artworks on the sides of empty freight cars sitting on side tracks.

I had a friend named Chuck who grew up in an eastern Oregon town called Culver. An agricultural hamlet, its main crop was spearmint. In the 1970s, he used to hang out in the area around the train station when he visited his merchant marine father while he waited to ship back out. Chuck took me to those childhood haunts that remained when I lived in the Pacific Northwest from the mid-1980s to 1992. A surprising number were still in operation, their Rainier Beer and Henry Weinhard neon signs glowing in their dirty windows and turning the faces of the occupants into hues of ghastly blues, yellows, greens and reds. They were mostly bars and pool halls. There was also a Salvation Army where he ended up on occasion. The establishments reminded me of San Diego when I lived there in the fall and winter of 1978-1979. In other words, a sailor's paradise. Tattoo parlors (before tattoos were cool), sex workers who called themselves hookers, and lots of dive bars full of smoke, body odor, sadness, broken men and desires. And women I sometimes thought wondered what the fuck they were doing there. When I went to these places, the cheap beer tasted good, as it might in a Tom Waits song. You know, down there by the train. Or a Bukowski screed. Or a blues tune composed from a place in the human soul where nothing good remains, the scars of the past inflamed by cotton dust and the dirt of Parchman Farm. Blues so dirty not even Pat Boone could clean them up. Floors soaked in the piss of thousands over decades. Warm beer and mean women for those of us with nowhere else to stay.

The train stopped. I found my way to the door, got off and headed to the waiting area in front of the station. Stephanie arrived a couple of minutes later, and drove me north through Portland. I watched the city pass by while we began to catch up on things that had occurred since my last visit. Text messages, emails and phone calls can not make up for in-person conversation. Faces can say so many things technology cannot transmit. Eyes are windows to certain emotional truths, at least in my experience. Our particular friendship is one that began in the late 1980s. It's a testimony to our tenacious tending of it that it remains; through love in its multiple forms and meanings, making and raising children, age and distance. Her passion is food. Growing it, cooking it, keeping it affordable for all. Indeed, her conversations on the subject always refine and redefine my perception of that essential element of human life.

We stopped at the food co-op where she has worked for most of the past thirty years. It's a completely vegetarian store nestled in a neighborhood in Portland's Southeast. Known as the People's Food Coop, it has been hosting a farmer's market every Wednesday for as long as I can remember. Even though the weather was a bit on the cold side, this Wednesday was no different. Perhaps fifteen vendors stood in the cold parking lot hoping the rain that threatened would hold off until they closed up shop. Mostly what I saw for sale were fungi, small greens, dried chile peppers, warm soups and pastries. Stephanie stopped at a few of the stalls, conversing with the vendors about their farms and their wares. A guy named Nigel who was selling dried chiles was someone I first met on a book tour for my book on the Weather Underground. He was managing an anarchist community space and bookshop at the time. The year was 1998. He and I reminisced for a few minutes about the event and then talked about politics and our lives since the last time we saw each other. The event had been disrupted by a fellow on a bicycle who began yelling at me, calling me a mass murderer and despot because I had written the book. At first, Nigel and I addressed his accusations with a certain seriousness, but when it became clear his only intention was to disrupt the event, a few younger folks in the audience worked with Nigel and got the bicyclist out of the building. The event continued without any further problems. After buying some mushrooms from another vendor and some beer from the store, Stephanie and I got back into the car and continued on.

The city rolled on by through the passenger side window. I watched newly gentrified blocks followed by empty shells of buildings and people on the streets riding bicycles, walking, smiling, yelling. Remnants of the 2020 police riots sprinkled the landscape; the aforementioned graffiti, charred fences and burn marks on the outside of a building or two, and some police stations enclosed by chain link fencing. We arrived in northeast Portland at the house she shares with a couple folks, one a longtime friend of hers (and father to their children) and the other a co-worker.

The former, Andy K, is a sculptor. Art is his entry to this world. It is a key element of his identity. He's one of those cats who comes at the political world with a healthy skepticism. I don't know that he would even identify his understanding as political, given his rejection of labeled ideologies. Unlike others who approach it that way, this didn't seem to lead him to despair or a deadening cynicism. Instead, his questions became more radical, as in getting to the root. Our conversations centered around the role of art and the nature of language. A good example of his meaning is how we tend to separate ourselves into us and them. There is no other. There's just us.

As we wandered the nearby neighborhoods, Andy provided me with a historical overview of the turf we were walking on. He told me about raves on the top of a mountain called Rocky Butte as we

walked around the small park at its top. He took me to a traditional Catholic shrine with statuary right out of the pictures of saints on the holy cards we were given in Catholic elementary school. Offi-

cially known as the National Sanctuary of Our Sorrowful Mother, it is commonly referred to as The Grotto. It's a place where Catholic saints are manipulated and sold by the commercial element of the Church while nuns and others take care of the sanctuary's physical well-being. The shrine reminded me of Lourdes and other such manifestations of Catholic spirituality and over-the-top piety; its combination of suffering and beauty as the ultimate realization of how most Catholics perceive their faith. Andy speculated that this place was one of those earthly spots where the transcendent became three-dimensional, and the Catholic Church had claimed it and made it their own; a point of energy, if you will. Before the missionaries and their lot arrived, perhaps the native Chinook and other nations knew of and respected its spiritual uniqueness in their own way. We walked along a bike path near I-205 that wandered by an urban farm inhabited by goats and chickens. The building seemed to be a squat. Nearby was another shrine, erected to a couple who had died. While we took in this shrine, a group of women living in the subsidized housing nearby came out to smoke cigarettes. They assumed we were city workers and asked if we were "going to get rid of the eyesore." I told them no. I didn't bother telling them I didn't consider it to be an eyesore. In fact, in my mind it is a remarkable piece of folk art. They returned to their smokes. A houseless couple smoked a joint nearby, their possessions in a pile beside them.

Despite the pressures from police, property owners and the nature of their lives in general, those without houses seem to have been incorporated more into the social structure of some US cities and towns. Their tents and other shelters have diminished their presence in more public areas, but the numbers of panhandlers seems about the same as a few years ago when I last traveled. It was a fellow on the corner of 102nd Ave and Glisan in Portland that brought this home to me. He stood at a traffic light, holding his sign asking for change. At the same time he sprinkled sunflower seeds on the sidewalk. Pigeons flew down from their perches on electric wires and in trees, pecking at the food. The fellow put his arm out and three or four pigeons flew up and alighted there. I figured he must have lived in the area for a while to have that familiarity with birds known for their mistrustful nature.

After a couple days in Portland, Stephanie and I headed north to Olympia, Washington. That's where we met more than thirty years ago. I had moved up from Oakland with my son, his mother Holly, and our friend Chuck. That was in 1985. The shift from the city of Oakland to the woods of the Olympic Peninsula was both welcome and life-changing. The first few months we spent living near a lake. Fields of daffodils bloomed in March. Wild animals walked by the single-wide trailer we shared with Chuck. The woodstove kept the damp of the morning fog and the Washington rain away. Stephanie had moved from the Chicago area to attend college. I met her at the school's daycare center where she worked and my son attended while his mother went to class and I worked. Our circle of mutual friends widened when I went back to the same college to get a bachelor's degree. We became friends, and have remained so.

The drive from Portland to Olympia isn't a particularly long one. Straight up I-5. I continued to marvel at how damp the weather was, even for the traditionally damp Pacific Northwest. Rain beat steadily on the windshield for the first hour. When we were just south of Mt. Saint Helen, the sun broke through, warming both of our faces. It didn't last. By the time we were passing through Centralia, the rain had returned. The Wobbly martyrs whose blood had long washed away since they were massacred that Armistice Day in 1919 knew the climate well. Their blood may have returned to the earth, but their story lives. I believe there is even an official monument to them and the occurrences of that day now. Centralia is a mix of right wing white folks, many Latinos, and a few refugees from the gentrifying town of Olympia some thirty or so miles north. The clouds covered the tops of the mountains. Mt. Saint Helen's peak was invisible and Mt. Rainier's even more so given the distance from the highway. When we stopped at a rest stop, I couldn't help but notice the smell of decaying timber. It is in the temperate rain forests of this region where one is pretty much forced to acknowledge the natural cycle of birth-growth-death-de-

74

cay and rebirth. One's senses allow no other possibility. If you don't see the dead tree limbs and stumps rotting almost before your eyes, you can't help but smell the pungent odor of decay. Various fungi and mosses grow on most organic matter. The omnipresent emerald luminescence of the vegetation soothes ones eyes, its greenness a natural pacifier. It's not unpleasant, just a reminder of who really manages the show humans think they control. There's a song by the Grateful Dead that includes a line poetically describing the vegetative circle from seed to bloom to decay. That line describes the essence of the Pacific Northwest rain forest. Bloom and decay, lots of decay.

Everywhere one goes in the USA one sees the same stores. Owned by corporate structures almost too grand to comprehend, these stores include many more commercial identities than the well-known megaliths like Walmart and Amazon, even though they might be owned by the same banks and humans. They certainly share corporate board members somewhere in the web such relationships involve and depend on. The Pacific Northwest's Fred Meyer's chain is one such entity. Founded by a young German immigrant who sold coffee from a cart, it is now one of the larger regional chains of so-called hypermarket superstores in the region. Despite its size, it merged with Kroger's in 1998. In 2022, Kroger merged with Albertsons. Towards the end of the same year, Kroger announced it would be buying Albertsons outright. Who knows which corporate or Wall Street monster will consume it or be consumed by it next? Ken Kesey once told Paul Krassner in an interview that everything leads back to the Bank of America. While not true in a literal sense, it's certainly true in a metaphorical and figurative one. Everything does lead back to the banks and the boards that run them, especially in the USA. Money fucks up everything. Many of us know this while we get sucked into its vortex no matter how strong our resistance.

My son has a Master's in Urban Planning. His focus is on public transit, but one of the things Julian Agyeman — the man who ran the program he was in — writes about is food sustainability and its meaning, especially as it regards creating and maintaining genuinely democratic urban communities. In his book *Introducing Just Sustainabilities*, Agyeman presents the issues involved in the world of food access and sustainability, specifically as to how they relate to other social justice movements more focused on race and class. In the process, he provides an important, essential and convincing challenge to modern sustainability movements and their approach to questions of race and class. I thought of Agyeman in the discussions about food that Stephanie and I had during the week we were hanging out. Her understanding that access to good and healthy food should not be dependent on one's income is part of what informs her interest in the topic. It's an understanding that goes beyond recipes and the healthiness of individual foods. The understanding she operates with sees human consumption and distribution of food in a grander historical and economic context that centers it in the history of human existence. Food, like art, is political. Hell, everything is political, whether we like it or not. It's just a question of which politics we will take as our own: those that favor the existing unequal structures, or those that challenge them. I still believe that pretending politics doesn't matter means the person doing so has accepted the existing structures by default. The historian Howard Zinn said it like this: "You can't be neutral on a moving train."

When we arrived in Olympia, we parked the car using one of those parking apps. Just one more means of collecting data yet described as a convenience. Then we ate at a favorite bakery of ours we were both surprised was still in business. The food was as good as we remembered it. The pastries were European in style, with an emphasis on German strudel and torts. I told Stephanie how my son, Ian, and I would stop at the bakery every day on our walk home from his school. The pastries gave both of us the sugar rush we needed to send us down the sidewalk. I also quietly recalled a couple of visits she and I had made. Still, the moment I remember best occurred in front of those strudel and danishes on January 16, 1991. Ian and I were on our way home as usual. We stopped in the bakery, ordered our usual treat and waited for the young woman at the counter to complete the transaction. A radio was playing music — probably some kind of pop music. The news came on at the top of the hour. It began with the sound of explosions and a reporter telling the world that the explosions being heard were broadcast from Baghdad, Iraq. The United States had just begun its attack; an attack three thousand people in Olympia had just protested against the day before. The clerk set the bag containing the pastries on the counter and grabbed my hand when I handed her the dollar bills in exchange. Tears streamed down her cheeks. I held her hand for three or four minutes before she let go. After wiping her face with a napkin, she whispered thanks. I smiled and said goodbye. Ian took my hand and we left. I went to a phone booth and began the phone tree our antiwar group had set up to respond to just such an attack.

The bakery was near the Greyhound station, now boarded up and abandoned. When I lived in Olympia, the Greyhound was often my means to get to Seattle. It was also the scene of a couple rowdy protests during the company bus drivers' strike that began in 1990, a strike precipitated by the ownership of Greyhound selling the company to a hedge fund that proceeded to destroy much of the company in order to give its shareholders big returns on their money. Of course, that meant the hedge fund managers would be going after the bus drivers' union. This was and is a classic tactic by those who make their money by buying other corporate entities, selling off those entities' infrastructure, laying off their employees and then selling the stock at a higher rate than its true value. The sell-off is possible because the destruction of the company creates a false and temporary profit even though the company no longer exists. Naturally, the attack on the drivers and their union provoked a bitter and occasionally violent strike by the drivers. At the Olympia bus station, our strike support group sat in front of buses driven by scab drivers because the drivers themselves were forbidden to do so by the courts. The cops cleared us away over and over. In Seattle, at least one striking driver was hit and killed by a scab driver. The criminals who were buying and selling the company took their profits to the bank.

Stephanie and I checked in with the people where we were staying, and then walked downtown. After some looking around in a couple of vintage clothing stores, we found a bookstore. Cozy and out of the rain, we spent an hour there among its blend of books, quietude and political posters. A cat who lived in the store watched us from its various perches. Later that evening we drank beer at a local pub. Some things are the same no matter where you go. Drinking beer at pubs is one such thing; only the decor, conversation and the brewers change. While in Folsom, my brother, his wife and I hit a couple of pubs. We drank different brews, and talked shit. While in Olympia, Stephanie and I hit the one pub, drank brews and talked. In our wandering over the next couple days, I was reminded that Olympia remains a simmering station of wealth and greed, poverty, racism and an anarchism peculiar to the region. It's an anarchism that is always radical and often analytical; its presence in local movements of resistance is usually greater than any I've encountered anywhere else in northern America. The ongoing gentrification of the port of Olympia is as blatant as the hatred the police have for the anarchists, especially those organizing and providing mutual aid for the numbers of unhoused in the city. Likewise, it is equivalent in the distrust the anarchists have for government and NGO-generated programs their authors claim will help those on the streets.

As for the Olympia port, lots that used to house warehouses, random discount stores, auto repair shops and bakeries were now the foundation for luxury hotels interspersed with upscale bakeries, restaurants, boutiques and some affordable housing plots. One holdover from the port's past is the Olympia Farmers Market, now year-round and thriving. Our Saturday began with breakfast with friends at one of those bakeries. Meanwhile, the weather remained chilly and wet. The benefit of this unusual weather is the blanket of green across this piece of earth. The downside is one felt mostly by the poor, whose lodgings suffer from a lack of appropriate insulation, leaky roofs or who have no lodgings at all. Regarding the latter, this means they are unable to sleep and their encampments are gone. Shelters provide shelter for some, but for others, the weather means walking in the rain for hours on end and catching sleep in doorways or the public library when they can.

Survival is one big reason why humanity is so creative. From the discovery of fire to the invention of tools and onward to the building of communities and societies, the survival of the species is the foundation of these endeavors. Likewise, it could be our downfall, given that the powerful among us tend to manipulate these tools of survival to their benefit, rejecting the concept of sharing in favor of hoarding. When push comes to shove, they would kill off most of humanity if they believed doing so would ensure their survival. Those of us who struggle against that power understand this, even if we express it in less cosmic terms. Those who hold that power know exactly what they are doing and very few of them have many, if any, qualms about their mission. Indeed, the environment is political. The fact of conquest made it so. The conqueror has changed his language and, in places like the United States, made his means of control so sophisticated we often participate willingly in it. However, as the violence of the police and military reminds us, brutality is the essence of that control. Our lives are always informed by this understanding, no matter whether we live them according to the rules or in opposition to them.

We awoke Sunday morning, knowing that we would be returning to Portland sometime that day. After a leisurely breakfast, we packed our backpacks and headed out. Since we were not in a hurry, Stephanie drove us through downtown Olympia and out onto East Bay Drive to one of the town's more rural areas. Smoke from wood stoves mixed with the drizzle and fog hanging over the assorted homes and small barns that populated the areas not dominated by new and probably expensive condo developments and fundamentalist churches. Although this part of Washington had a fair number of such churches when I lived there in the late 1980s and early 1990s, the number of such places had jumped incredibly, if not exponentially, since then. The dominant color of the environs was still green. No amount of herbicide and holy water is going to keep the process of nature's moss and mold from asserting its place in the natural scheme of things. The big trees will continue to grow, die and decay much longer than the men and women masquerading as their god's spokespeople will spread their gospels and fleece their flocks, even if their flocks want to be fleeced, which it seems is the case. I suppose the sense of security and righteousness is worth whatever one is asked to pay for those searching for such phenomena. It's not that I'm against gods, but when people cash in on them, I walk in the opposite direction. I'm just not buying it.

After a shopping trip to one of the food co-ops in Olympia, Stephanie put the car back on I-5 heading south. The weather was dry, but still cold. We stopped at a rest stop to stretch our legs. Our conversation was about music, art, our friendship and how I wanted to spend the next couple days before I headed back to Vermont. I didn't have any particulars in mind, but I did hope to spend many of the remaining hours with her. On the last day of my visit, we walked south thirty or so blocks to Portland's Mount Tabor Park. A pleasantly wooded area with well kept paths and many residents walking and biking on those paths, the park provides some great views of the city. After walking for an hour or so, we found a bench in the sun where we sat soaking in the diminishing warmth. Once that disappeared, we ambled back through the neighborhood to her home. It was rush hour in the city and the wait to cross certain east-west boulevards was longer than it had been on the way to Mount Tabor. Since neither of us was in a hurry, this was not a problem.

While we wandered through the streets, Stephanie told me a tragic story of an encounter she had while riding her bicycle to work on the same streets. As she rode, she saw a car screech to a stop on one of the main avenues; someone inside opened a rear door and threw a woman onto the road. The woman was covered in blood. Stephanie stopped her bike and went over to the woman, who told Stephanie to go away. Instead, Stephanie tried to help her. Still, the woman rejected her help while also telling her thank you. Eventually, the injured woman left the road. It seemed to be one of those situations where the person needing assistance was unable or unwilling to acknowledge it, their fear and emotional state preventing coherent thinking. Stephanie never saw her again. It was a brutal reminder of the random, impersonal nature of the capitalist city. While I was there I heard about a plan to install hidden microphones in certain areas of Portland. These devices would be monitored by the police. The authorities' reasoning behind this intrusion was that they could then respond to gunfire incidents more quickly. Instead of waiting for a resident to call in such an incident, the transmissions from the hidden microphones would ostensibly pinpoint the location and cops could be sent there quickly. Of course, these microphones were supposed to be installed first in neighborhoods that were mostly working class and Black, Latino and indigenous. Talk about Big Brother bullshit. The authorities are even claiming it's for the residents' own good. To me, it sounds like another step toward the panopticon already near completion in places like the Palestinian areas of Jerusalem and throughout the Occupied Territories. As a general rule, law enforcement installs surveillance devices to protect class interests, not the interests of those they are surveilling. This seems especially true in the United States, Britain, parts of China and Israel.

The remainder of my time before I was driven to the airport was spent conversing with Stephanie and her housemates and playing a game similar to Scrabble. It was clear to me from the way they excelled in it that Stephanie and Andy played this game quite often. My plane from Portland to Newark, New Jersey left on time. It was what is called a red-eye flight. Once the passengers were settled, I fell asleep for most of the flight. It landed at 7:30 AM New

Jersey time the next day. I spent the next four hours in the airport terminal, ordering and paying for breakfast with an app on my phone, then falling asleep for a little less than an hour. I was back in Vermont by 1:00 PM east coast time. My housemate picked me up and I went home to read mail, say hello to the cat, and sleep.

My next journey took place in March 2023. I was heading to Texas. The first thing I noticed stepping off the plane in Austin was the warm temperature. The winter in Vermont and much of the north had been unusual, mostly because the bulk of the snow fell much later than most previous winters. So, it was barely above freezing when I left Burlington the afternoon of March 13th and it was near 70° Fahrenheit that evening in Austin. My body appreciated the change.

One of the first things I noticed on the drive from the airport to my friend David's house was that Austin was quite built up from when I was here in the 1980s. Towers of glass, steel and a composite of other man-made materials impose their shadows on the town, keeping the multitude of one story burger joints and taco shops in the shade. At the same time it has miles and miles of bike and hiking trails, lots of trees and parks along the Colorado River and the main lake in the city. Although there are lots of yuppie types, there are also lots of what some still call hippies of all ages, and punks. There are at least three food co-op stores, several for-profit health food stores and an incredible variety of restaurants, from taco stands to BBQ, vegan/vegetarian breakfast, and high-end places. The street I hung out on when I hitched through was Guadalupe Street. It was Austin's version of Berkeley's Telegraph Avenue, San Francisco's Haight-Ashury District or Washington D.C.'s M Street. In other words, it was where the freaks hung out. To my surprise, the street still had some of the buildings I remembered from my visits in the early 1980s. Of course, the businesses inside the stores were different, but skyscrapers had not yet replaced them. Thread-gills, where Janis Joplin sang before she moved to San Francisco, is no longer in business, but the building remains. Some of the graffiti on its sides reminds the world "Janis sang here." I had a buddy who ran away from his home in rural Texas in 1966 and began an ill-fated career selling marijuana on Guadalupe Street. He sold his first nickel bag there. By the early 1970s, he was moving hundreds of pounds through Texas from Mexico. Of course, he no longer hung out on the street. The DEA finally caught up with him in the early 1980s, despite his having changed his identity in the late 1970s. The last time I heard from him, he was on the run on his way to Vancouver, British Columbia. Later, a mutual friend told me the feds had finally caught up with him. I was told he got fifteen years in a federal pen.

According to various demographic surveys, Austin's population is about fifty percent white, thirty percent Latino and then lots of other folks including indigenous, African Americans, Africans and Asians. The unhoused population is nowhere as obvious as it is in California and the northwest. My guess is that it's better hidden. Perhaps those without a residence are able to hide their camps in the woods all over town or they have people whose couches they can crash on. The sheer monstrosity of the tall buildings downtown and the large numbers of new and expensive cars and trucks indicate that, as in most cities in the US, economic inequality defines the lives of most of its residents.

I stayed with a couple of friends while I was in town. David, who I have known for thirty years, moved there in the early years of the twenty-first century. The first day I was there, we met up with a friend of his who I knew through an email list she and I belong to. Made up of former student radicals at the University of Maryland, the list serves as a forum for reminiscence, political debate, name-calling and incendiary remarks designed to start an argument. Although almost all of the members of the list attended the university before my 1974-1975 year, many of their names were familiar to me. They were recent history when I was going to school there and some of them were still involved in political actions going on in the area; strikes, antiwar protests, and struggles around drug policy. Sue, who David and I met up with at a restaurant off of Guadalupe Street, was working as a clerk or something similar when the US invaded Cambodia at the end of April in 1970. She quit her job, divorced her husband who worked for the CIA, and jumped into the fray. She ended up being a member of a collective that produced a weekly leftist paper called the Washington Area Spark. The paper focused on local antiwar, anti-racist and labor struggles. Its archives are now online. Like thousands of others, she joined the new communist movement before the revolution got stifled by the State, circumstances and time. David listened while we shared stories about political actions, mutual

friends, and our lives up to that point. The beer was good and we were outside in the sun. As we talked, I thought about the hope we had back then. Was it due to our youth or was it just the zeitgeist of the time? By asking that question I knew its answer would be debated well past the time of our current conversation.

While she was alive, Lady Bird Johnson was the figurehead for a campaign to keep America beautiful. The campaign went national while her husband Lyndon was in the White House. I remember the billboards touting the slogan "Keep America Beautiful." Even in my ten year-old mind I wondered if they understood the irony of putting up ugly billboards urging US residents to keep the country beautiful. One of my favorite riffs on the campaign went like this: Keep America Beautiful, Get a Haircut!. Obviously, it was addressed to the growing number of young men and adolescent boys who were letting their hair grow long. The funny thing is that many older folks who hated long hair took up the slogan as a campaign. It seems rather ridiculous to most people now, but males with long hair truly offended many older people, especially older men, school principals and cops. I knew at least half a dozen guys who had had their hair shorn by cops and rednecks. My battle over hair length was more private. In other words, my dad and I argued over it until I left his house, but nobody outside those four walls cut a single strand.

Anyhow, the reason I mention Lady Bird and her campaign is because there are several parks near Austin named in her honor. One of them is a wildflower park and includes a few miles of trails, some playgrounds, and a gift shop. It is the arboretum of the University of Texas, and hosts various events much of the year. I spent the morning of my last full day in Texas with David and his family there. We wandered through the park; very few flowers were in bloom — mostly bluebonnets, which are native to Texas and are celebrated around the state. The grounds were beautiful and the park wasn't crowded. However, there was one section we found somewhat disconcerting, if not just plain repulsive.

This area featured various oak trees native to Texas. The trees were grown from acorns of oak trees the sponsors of the exhibit considered important in Texan history. White invader Texan history that is. Next to each tree was a plaque describing the importance of the tree in this version of history. Some were relatively harmless: preachers spreading the Baptist version of Jesus, or a schoolhouse that began under the tree. However, most of them described the massacre of Comanches, the institution of the so-called Texas Republic — which was nothing more than a temporary state of affairs enforced by US invaders determined to make Texas a slaveholding state, and the slaughter of more indigenous people in the occupation of their lands by white settlers/colonizers, and the US Army. David and I came up with a name for this history: Critical Racist Theory. Theory critical to racists. The fact it was there wasn't surprising, given the recent history of Texas. Furthermore, the history it told is a history too many US citizens consider as objective; the killing of indigenous people is just one of those things that makes this country great after all. What is disturbing is that this part of the gardens isn't challenged or amended to include the perspectives of those Texans opposed to the concept of white supremacy and who don't consider this version of history to be a complete history, since it only tells the conquerors' side.

Speaking of these Texans, many of them live in Austin. This helps explain, at least in part, the existence of a radical bookstore and the dynamic public library system in that city. One of the folks I met during this visit was a fellow who manages one of the branches in the system. As a recently retired library worker myself, it was nice to run into him and talk shop, as it were. After discussing the various computer systems and databases he worked with, we began talking policy. It was good to hear that the book banning craze favored by the

repressive religious right was not as successful in Austin as in other parts of Texas and the rest of the US South. Still, it was beyond anything I had experienced in my work in academic libraries and public libraries in Vermont. Library workers who stand up for the right to read whatever the hell people want to read are mostly unsung heroes in the United States. There are right-wing reasons for getting rid of libraries. Suppressing freedom of thought is at the top of the list.

It was the summer of 1982. The heat was intense. I stood on the side of some highway in Kansas, heading east. Behind me were uncountable acres of farmland covered in corn. The stalks were mostly above my head. In front of me were miles and miles of flatland covered in more corn. The farmer's son who had just dropped me off had talked about how before the farmers had taken over most of the land, much of the acreage had been covered in prairie grass. In fact, he told me that prairie grass had covered much of the Midwest from Oklahoma to the Dakotas. It was nature's way of preventing the topsoil from being blown away in the wind and thunderstorms that crossed the region. Corn did not perform the same function, especially since it was harvested and mowed every year. In fact, the farmer's son told me, it was the destruction of the prairie grass that had been partly responsible for the devastation caused by the Dust Bowl; you know, he said, the one Woody Guthrie sang about.

Ronald Reagan had been president for a little more than a year. The immediate future was obvious and it wasn't something I was looking forward to. I saw the recession deepening while the bulk of voting citizens blamed the growing number of poor for their fate. The number of middle fingers shown to me while I hitchhiked on interstates and country highways was on the increase. My beard was as dirty as my jeans and any peace I found on the road was rare compared to a mere three years earlier. At least I wasn't in Central

America, where it looked like Reagan and his fascist crew were pre-
paring to seek some serious revenge.

A truck pulled over to the shoulder behind me. I grabbed my bed-
roll and pack and ran to the passenger door. The driver wore a straw
hat and was as red as a dead lobster in the pot. He told me to hop
in and grab a beer from the cooler. I took his advice. Lefty Frizell
was playing on the radio. The song was "Long Black Veil." I remem-
bered because a boss I had when I worked at the military commis-
sary in Frankfurt played it all the time on his cassette player. I liked
his voice. We rode into Kansas City, drinking and talking shit. He
dropped me off near where the Kansas City Royals play. The Royals
were on the road so there was no game going on. We sat in the stadi-
um parking lot and finished off the remaining beers. It was early and
he was heading into town to see a girl. I wished him luck and he said
goodbye. I spent the night sleeping in some bushes. I was awakened
by a couple of stadium security guys who bought me breakfast and
sent me on my way. Life was good. Reagan could go fuck himself.

There's a certain beauty to the Midwest. The open vistas with
roads straighter than Christian pastors pretend to be inviting the
traveler to continue into the horizon. Of course, it's a horizon one
never reaches but then again never cares that they don't. The birds
appear in huge flocks above the earth when one comes upon a pond
or lake. The heron looks beyond the human intruder, a fish in its
mouth and an eye out for danger. Then it spreads its wings, flying off
as beautiful as any eagle or hawk. Its predation is subtle, unlike those
cousins of theirs. Then there's the sudden buildup of storms that dis-
solve in a cacophony of lightning and thunder. The amber waves of
grain are like elements of a painting.

Almost forty years later I was back in the middle of the USA. As
the song says, train kept a'rollin. My train departed in the morning
from downtown Austin. I'm writing this on the train from Austin

to Chicago in 2023. I'm thinking about Bob Dylan's song "The Ballad of Hollis Brown." You know, the song where he sings about a farmer with a bunch of kids who has pretty much lost everything. The rats have got his flour, bad blood his mare, and the well is dry. Seven shotgun shells, one for each member of his family. If you don't know the song, you can guess the rest. It isn't wholesome or pretty. Oklahoman Leon Russell did a great version of it with the Gap Band, who were also from Oklahoma. John Mellencamp had a pretty decent song on a similar theme called "Paper and Fire." The song featured some great fiddle playing. It was the 1980s when he released it, and the Wall Street vultures were peeling away the entrails of the agricultural carrion otherwise known as the family farm. Tractors and everything else went up for sale. Banks and auctioneers were making lots of money. The humans who worked the farms joined the army, or hit the food shelves. Anger was on the program, but Ronnie Reagan's shit-eating grin, his henchmen and women in Congress and a few other assorted official scumbags convinced the farmer he was going to be okay, despite all the evidence to the contrary. When he was president, Reagan was called the great communicator by much of the US media. What they really meant was that he was a really good liar. It was as if one didn't believe his lies, it was because they were against America.

Mark Twain wrote about one of his journeys across the country in the book *Roughing It*. In previous trips, I did my share of roughing it. Having a relatively comfortable seat in a train is quite a luxury as far as I'm concerned. I want to say roughing it is for the young people, but there are way too many older folks who have no other choice today. The arrogance and insensitivity in such a statement is not something I would want to claim.

The Midwest is what many of us think of when we think about being "American." The region was born from the misnamed Indian wars whose sole purpose was to forcibly take land from the people who had lived there for centuries. That conquest played out into the twentieth century in many parts of this middle west. Presidents, emperors and their sidekicks bought and sold land they never really owned. The greatest of these land sales was the one we call the Louisiana Purchase. The US army and the settlers pushed their way across the grasslands, mountains, deserts and bluffs, co-conspirators in a plan that involved land theft and the death or imprisonment of thousands. For several decades thereafter, these plains contained farms farmed by white folks descended from other white folks from the Eastern US and Europe. Although few slaves worked the land here, the battle over slavery helped determine the regional alignments. Missouri was a slave state while Kansas wasn't. Both were scenes of violence for and against slavery. When Kansas territory was opened up (after being taken from the peoples native to the region and other indigenous nations living there that had already been ethnically cleansed from lands further east), slavers and the politicians that served them sent roughnecks and other mercenary types into the territories to harass and intimidate abolitionists who were settling there. Many of the abolitionists came from the east intending to be the majority when the decision to declare Kansas' status as free or slave. It was all part of a devilish deal made in Washington called the Missouri Compromise. The abolitionists from the East built up the town of Lawrence only to see much of it burned to the ground by pro-slavery elements. In response, John Brown, one of slavery's most committed foes, led his abolitionist band on a raid in Osawatomie and killed a group of slavery supporters. The battle lines were drawn. The sometimes terrible swift sword of justice was soon to launch a conflagration of hellish proportions that would end chattel slavery in the United States, but not the battle over what it meant to those who lost that conflict or the

91

white supremacist consciousness that it both fostered and was fostered by. What an ugly history.

The train I was riding, called the Texas Eagle, did not go through Kansas. We rode through Arkansas and Missouri instead. I arrived at the Austin station about an hour before its scheduled departure only to discover that the train was delayed. Someone had jumped in front of the engine right after it left San Antonio. Was it suicide by train engine? The stationmaster could not (or would not) reveal the fate of that individual, but the delay meant I could find a coffee shop and a grocery store while we waited to board. I found both within a mile and proceeded to get a cup of coffee, breakfast and a sandwich for later. Train food is not the best; it's mostly pre-packaged and microwaved. The day had begun on the chilly side, but by the time the Texas Eagle came into the station, the sun was shining and the platform was warming up.

The conductor scanned the ticket on my phone and told me where I would be sitting. I boarded the train, went upstairs and found a seat. A young woman with a blonde braid cascading down her slender back sat down next to me. As the train pulled out of the station we began conversing. She was in town for a music and arts festival known as South by Southwest or SXSW. Her two-piece combo had performed in a couple venues and now she was heading to Dallas to meet up with a deejay friend. As she put it, she was just tagging along. We talked about her music. She told me her voice was her primary instrument and that she composed most of her group's music by vocalizing lines and harmonies which she recorded. Then, she manipulated the sounds on mixing software to create a song. Ultimately, she told me that different musicians would take the arrangement she created and transcribe the parts onto their own instruments. I listened to a couple of songs she was working on. Then she fell asleep. I watched Texas roll on by; camps of the unhoused were set up next to auto junkyards. Men and women sitting around small fires warming their food, their bodies wrapped in sleeping bags and blankets. Tin and aluminum cans littered the camps, broken and smashed cars littered the junkyards. Camps of the unhoused are the American truth the glitz of Austin's shiny highrises is supposed to hide.

Among the couple of dozen folks who got on in Dallas was a guy wearing a brown felt hat, a plaid woolen jacket, blue jeans and boots. His white ponytail draped down his back a few inches and he was talking with a couple of Black women while he settled in. They talked and laughed for an hour or so until the women fell asleep. Then he turned to me. We got to talking and eventually he pulled a bottle of tequila out of his pack. We sipped on the bottle; him more than me. I'm not much of a tequila drinker. The taste never appealed to me. As the train rambled on and the dusk turned to darkness, he told me his story. To begin with, he said he was high on mushrooms. One of the women he had been talking with when he boarded had traded him some mushrooms for a couple of THC gummies. Then, I heard the story of his life. A champion state wrestler in high school, he got a scholarship to Texas A&M which he blew off after his freshman year. After working here and there for a bit, he joined the Navy. He had tried to get into the Marines but they wouldn't take him. I suggested that might have been a lucky break for him, but he disagreed. I heard a couple of his Navy stories and then we began discussing music. Somehow, the name of Donald Trump came up. He looked me in the eye and told me he had me figured for a liberal. I ignored the comment and he said it again. I started talking about Stevie Ray Vaughn, whose statue David and I had seen on one of our hikes in an Austin park a couple days earlier. That got him off of politics.

I didn't really think much about why I decided to shift the subject away from politics until my editor mentioned it. I had grown up on military bases and was used to avoiding political discussions with people whose politics were on the other side of the spectrum from mine. It just wasn't worth it, especially when it came to the Vietnam War. In my experience one was either for it or against it. The one ongoing exception to that rule was my father. My reasons for avoiding such arguments included the belief that most people older than a certain age were usually pretty entrenched in their beliefs and therefore much harder to convince. Another was the idea that my time arguing would be better spent trying to convince the people sitting on the fence, so to speak. When Donald Trump was elected, there were people I considered friends and acquaintances supporting him. This included some of my relatives. I wasn't ready to push them out of my life—and I figured that my time would be better spent going after Trump than the people I cared about. So, once again, I became adept at changing the subject when politics came up.

Somehow, the subject of the THC gummies came back around. He asked if I wanted one and I said yes. After having been in states where marijuana was legal for the past few years it was weird to think that I was once again in a place where adults still got thrown in jail for the stuff. He told me he was on the run from the law. I wondered what he meant and was going to ask when he volunteered that he had a DWI that he didn't want to deal with. The court was demanding he go to AA meetings, install a breathalyzer device on his truck and pay thousands of dollars to attend classes about drinking. He decided to go to live on some land he owned in Michigan instead. Every time I heard one of these stories about getting busted for driving while intoxicated I am grateful I never got a license or drove. I can only imagine how much more I would have run into the law than I already had in my younger days. A little while later, I went back to my seat and fell asleep. The gummies helped that process tremendously.

I awoke just as the sun was rising. The sky was orange and the shadows across the land were dark. The train had filled up again overnight. The newest passengers included several young Amish families, a couple Latino families and several mostly older African-Americans. The woman running the cafe car waited until 7:00 AM before making her announcements. These included several jokes, mostly of the punny kind. I dug her attempt to keep it friendly and respected her ability to make most every one smile. There was a woman and her family who got on in Arkansas during the night. She spent the morning talking with her children and singing train songs by Johnny Cash, Gladys Knight; and Steve Goodman. "Folsom Prison Blues", "Midnight Train to Georgia", and "City of New Orleans". Her voice was a pleasant alto and she kept it at a low volume. She talked almost anytime she wasn't sleeping or singing. I learned through no intention of my own why she was traveling with her grandkids. Their mother had deserted them for another man and her son — their father — was working overtime in some factory to make up for it. As she told the conductor, at least the plant was paying him time and a half for all the overtime he was putting in. She said she was convinced the only reason they were doing so was to keep the union out. Her son had mentioned that union organizers were holding meetings. The conductor told her he hoped the union succeeded. She agreed, but admitted it made her nervous since Arkansas wasn't a union-friendly place and her son needed the fricking job. It was spring vacation for the grandchildren and they were on their way to visit family in Wisconsin while the son worked. The kids were occupied with reading and playing games, obviously used to their Grandma's loquacious and friendly nature. Tic tac toe and the card game called UNO. I overheard her telling one of the younger ones it was snowing in Chicago. Her granddaughter asked if that made things better or worse. I thought it was a good question. Grandma responded by saying it all depended on how much it snowed. She had a point.

The next big city we would go through was St. Louis, Missouri. As we approached from the south, I was reminded how much of that town was historically industrial in nature. Even in 2023 after decades of deindustrialization, there were still plenty of trains filled with materials and goods in the trainyards we rolled through. Smoke still poured from a few stacks, not as much as a few decades ago when I passed through last, but more than I expected. The Gateway Arch still lent its presence to downtown. It was hard to tell just passing through, but the city looked hollowed out. Many buildings that once housed hundreds of workers each were empty, their windows broken, their outside wiring and plumbing torn from their moorings, and camps of the unhoused occupying lots that once held automobiles for three shifts of industrial workers. A young man sitting next to the Texan fellow I had been talking with the night before was getting off the train at St. Louis. The Texan and he had been discussing music for a while. Both extolled the playing of John Coltrane, Miles Davis and Buddy Guy. The young man and his saxophone were going to a band festival there. As we traveled very slowly through the railyards, the grandmother pointed out a train carrying coal. It's a coal train, said one of her grandchildren. The young man with the sax laughed. Coltrane, he said. That's what my sax likes to play.

I don't know a lot about St. Louis. Chuck Berry, Ike and Tina. The lines from Johnny Cash's "Big River". Anheuser Busch and the St. Louis Cardinals baseball team. Lou Brock, Curt Flood and Bob Gibson. Stan Musial and Tim McCarver. They beat the Boston Red Sox in the 1967 World Series. The Red Sox beat them in their championship contests in the twenty-first century. Budweiser is both the best-selling beer and, as far as I'm concerned, the worst tasting. The brewery switched to using rice instead of barley for the primary grain during World War Two as part of some restrictions on barley related to wartime needs. That switch forever defined the taste of Budweiser's so-called King of Beers. I knew a Jesuit seminarian when I lived in Frankfurt am Main who grew up in St. Louis. He ended up being a labor and tenant organizer while in college. Then he decided to become a Jesuit. I don't know if he stuck it out to become a priest, but I do remember he would let us use the seminary's mimeograph machine to print antiwar leaflets we passed out to the GIs on base there.

The train took its time chugging through the railyards of the city. The Mississippi River ran next to the track and then the Missouri. Empty freight cars sat on side tracks, the graffiti on their sides the only thing that wasn't dingy. Various workers stood around or drove machinery and a light snow fell. Occasionally, our train pulled over to a siding while a (usually) long freight train went by. The reason for these delays is that in the United States freight trains have the right of way. It has something to do with the ownership of the tracks. The only exception to this that I know of is in the north-eastern US. In that region Amtrak pays the freight companies for the right of way. Most of the freight trains I saw go by while we sat at one siding or another were carrying foodstuffs and lumber. There were a couple that had different loads. One extremely long train was made up of dozens of flatcars carrying various military vehicles — Strykers, jeeps, Humvees and two-and-a-half ton utility vehicles. Another long train was made up almost entirely of tanker cars; some had symbols on their sides revealing the flammability of the contents. Other cars had various hazardous material symbols that I could not decipher. I wished I had my daughter to identify them. She knew all of those signs when she was younger. She shared that knowledge whenever we were on the highway. Her knowledge reminded me how much toxic shit is on the highways every day. The recent surge in freight train derailments only makes one more aware of how much is also traveling by rail. There was a time in Germany when anti-nuclear activists had set up a warning system that was activated any time a train carrying nuclear materials was traveling. Once activated, folks would arrive at the tracks and attempt to block the train. Sometimes they were successful. The closest such actions in recent years would be the attempts to block pipelines in Canada and the US led by indigenous people whose lands were in the paths of those pipelines. Other relatively recent actions that qualified were the attempts in Olympia and Tacoma, Washington to stop military equipment being loaded onto ships bound for Iraq and that US-managed debacle.

About half of the passengers disembarked at the station and were replaced with an equal number of people getting on. The train remained full. I fell back asleep soon after leaving St. Louis. When I awoke we were in the prairie. Small towns went by. Trucks and tractors in the fields in between the towns were visible in the distance. The grandmother taking her grandchildren to Wisconsin continued her monologue and the pony-tailed Texan was sharing what he considered wisdom with the passenger who had replaced the young man with the saxophone. I heard bits and pieces of their speech, but mostly their voices droned in the background. Looking out at the vast and level land surface through the train windows, I was once again reminded of the story about the prairies that the pickup truck driver had told me so long ago. The one about how the prairies used to be covered by prairie grass. It seems worth repeating. This grass kept the soil where it was. As the people we call settlers and sodbusters moved westward, that grass was replaced with crops like wheat and corn, both of which were harvested and neither of which prevented erosion like the wild prairie grass which had preceded them. My great uncle who lived north of the Twin Cities in Minnesota used to tell us kids stories about how his farm looked when he moved there as a child with his parents. He talked about the prairie grass too.

As we approached Joliet, Illinois I thought about the prisons there. Although it is the original prison that most people are familiar with thanks to the Blues Brothers movie, it is the prison actually called Stateville Correctional Center I was thinking of. I knew it was one of the first so-called Supermax prisons built in the United States. Essentially a torture chamber, these institutions are designed to turn humans into shadows of their former selves. Like the prisons in upstate New York, the prisons in and around Joliet are major employers in the region. This fact defines the politics and cultures of these areas in a certain way. Indeed, they make Bob Dylan's observation that the world is a big prison where some are prisoners and some are guards all too true. In other words, since both prisoners and prison staff are under lock and key, they are all in prison; a situation that cannot help but taint their consciences and their consciousness. I have a lawyer friend who works for a non-profit set up to provide legal aid for prisoners. He spends most of his time looking into prisoners' charges of abuse by guards. He's told me stories of the wounds he has seen and demanded explanations for. He also told me that he succeeds in getting reprimands for abusive guards about thirty percent of the time. Otherwise, they just get away with their abuse. Regarding the Bob Dylan observation above, I have noticed my friend's optimism about effective prison reform being replaced by an ugly cynicism over the years. His experience is but one example of what Bob Dylan was singing about. When I lived on the Olympic Peninsula in the town of Shelton, I occasionally partied with men who worked in the prison there. Most of them were Vietnam veterans who took the job because it was steady work and it paid well for the region at the time. Most of them also smoked a lot of weed (which was still a felony) and many of them were budding alcoholics. Of course, most had their own demons from their war experiences to deal with. The irony that they were smoking pot while they were guarding men — many of whom were in prison on marijuana charges — only intensified the truth of Dylan's lyric and the hypocrisy of the marijuana laws in particular.

After Joliet, Chicago is ahead. We rumbled towards the city district called the West Loop Gate neighborhood where the train station is located. Snow swirled in between the high-rise buildings. Steam rose from the streets. Idle train cars sat on sidings. Once I had disembarked, I went inside the station's Great Hall. It is a classic construction, high ceilings and benches like church pews. Truly majestic. I looked around for food and a beverage and discovered my choices were between a pizza joint and McDonald's. The pizza hit the spot: one slice of vegetarian and one slice of sausage. I headed towards the waiting room for my next ride — the Lake Shore Limited to Albany, New York. While I sat there, a young Black man came up to me. He was well-dressed in a striped polo shirt, a warm-looking Carhart coat and nice boots. He said hi and

told me he was heading home to Milwaukee. Then he told me he had just eaten some pills and asked if I could give him a couple dollars for a soda and chips from the nearby vending machines. I gave him a few dollars and he got his food. Then he started talking about his brother who was in real estate, and a sister who owned a hair salon. As he talked, the pills began to take effect. His words were slurred and he kept losing his train of thought. Soon he was nodding off. I kept him engaged for about twenty minutes until a young woman he was traveling with came back from the restroom and sat down next to him. I didn't want him to get busted for being high. I also wanted to make sure he wasn't going to overdose. I had grown all too familiar with the warning signs of opiate overdoses the last couple of years I worked in a public library. Opioids had become the apparent drug of choice (if opiates are ever a choice once one gets hooked) in the US population, and public libraries had become a place where people without anywhere else to go went after getting high. Some of them actually went to the library to inject their poison. Our staff training sessions began to include the treatment of overdoses and we were supplied with Narcan — an antidote to narcotics overdoses. I wandered off after his lady friend assured me she would make sure he got home. I had two more hours before my train departed. While I walked around the station I began noticing that many of the folks seemed to be dressed in clothes they had slept in. This got me thinking about the way people dressed along my journey so far. Those boarding in Texas tended to dress up a little. Not in suits or even jacket and ties, but at least in clean and new-looking clothes. Those in Arkansas, much less so. Grandma and her grandchildren were wearing sweatsuits that seemed to have permanent stains here and there. The folks getting on in St. Louis were dressed somewhat more neatly. Of course, the Amish passengers dressed like Amish dress whenever they are out in the world: coats, collared shirts and pressed pants for the men and boys, and dresses and bonnets for the women and girls. I wondered what these seemingly insignificant facts represented, if anything. Then my mind wandered away from passenger train fashion trends.

Around 8:40 PM, the first boarding announcement was made. It was for families and senior citizens. Although I rarely think of myself in that way (except when I get my social security check), I was pleasantly surprised when the station attendant told me to jump ahead, please sir. Being old is something I still don't think of as my situation. Hopefully, my physical well-being will continue to allow me the luxury of feeling younger than so many of my fellow older folks. While I walked down the boarding platform, I counted the cars on the train. The train I was boarding was sixteen coaches long, including the baggage and dining cars. The Texas Eagle had been a mere five coaches. As I walked toward the car I had been instructed to board, I heard Elvis Presley singing "Mystery Train" in

102

my head. Thank you very much. Train I ride, sixteen coaches long. Despite the Elvis in my brain, his version of the song is not my favorite. I think that would go to Paul Butterfield, Michael Bloomfield and the rest of that band on their self-titled album from 1965. It is one of Presley's best songs, though. Along with "Jailhouse Rock", "Little Sister", and "Suspicious Minds". Of course, that's just my opinion. Music, like all art, is a subjective thing.

After drinking a beer the first hour after the train left the station, I fell asleep. I woke up about an hour before dawn in western Pennsylvania. The early morning train was rolling on, stopping at stations seemingly without names; their signage not apparent in the dark. Conductors quietly communicated with each other and their dispatchers via traditional railroad signals, walkie-talkies and the occasional shout. Hardly anyone got on or off during this part of the ride. My recent travels told me that this seemed to be the case on the train lines that run more than once a day. However, those waiting to board one of the lines that only make three weekly trips often wait even when the train is two or more hours late. This was true on the leg of the journey from Austin to Chicago. Passengers had waited two and three hours after the scheduled arrivals for the Texas Eagle, which had been delayed just north of San Antonio.

We continued into Pennsylvania. It was a chilly morning out of Erie. There was a dusting of snow on the vineyards, of which there are many. The vineyards were something relatively new. They weren't there the last time I passed through Erie in 1981. I had been picked up by a biker driving an Econoline van. His Harley was in the back of the van. He was on his way to his parents, who lived in a double-wide trailer on the shore of Lake Erie. We stopped there and grilled some burgers, drank a few beers and conversed with his parents. There was a nuclear power plant in the distance, obviously using the lake waters to cool its turbines or whatever. Steam escaping through its stacks was visible from our vantage point more than fifty miles away. Eventually, he took me back out to the highway. I had eaten enough food to take me to my destination, which was my sister's house in Rochester, Minnesota. We smoked a joint of some Mexican weed and parted ways.

As we neared Albany, New York, college students emptied out of the train. The weekend I was traveling happened to be the end of spring break for many colleges in this part of the country. The conductor told me it was an easy time for him since most of them were both physically able to carry their own luggage and also smart enough to figure out where to get off the train. This wasn't always the case with older or less educated (or non-English speaking) passengers. Being back in the northeast, where marijuana is legal, I couldn't help but wonder if the conductor was stoned. His eyes were a bit glazed. When we pulled into Albany, the weather was sunny and maybe forty degrees. I was pleasantly surprised by the train station. It was spacious, clean, and had decent and affordable food and drink. There was even a post office inside. The station sat on the other side of the Hudson River in what is actually the town of Rensellaer, New York. The Mohawk River empties into the Hudson just a few miles north. Being a Sunday, the only businesses open were inside the station. I feel I lucked out being able to finish my journey on the Ethan Allen line from Albany to Burlington. This line, which was barely ten months old, provided me with a comfortable and easy way to get back home. The Burlington station is perhaps two and a half miles from my place. Like most of the previous stretch, the majority of the passengers on the Ethan Allen were college students. Fresh from the bosom of their homes, they seemed refreshed and ready to finish out their semester. I couldn't help but be reminded of my years working at college libraries. The burst of communal energy we always felt when the students and faculty came back from their spring break usually petered out a few days before exams. Then the cursing and anxiety set in. So did the number of students forsaking basic hygiene; their stress combined with coffee and adderal creating an odor not unlike that of a gym locker room.

Anyhow, the landscape passing by the Ethan Allen bore the marks of early spring in the north country. The grayness of the skies was broken only by the gray of bare trees poking their limbs in search of a non-existent sun. Piles of snow remained, their previous whiteness smudged by motor vehicle exhaust and dirt. I saw goats and a few cows in the fenced-in pastures, although most were probably inside barns keeping warm. There was an occasional whiff of manure as the day warmed to around fifty degrees, and released the odors of the farm. After living in the very similar to upstate New York climate of Vermont for a couple of decades, one becomes familiar with the rhythms of nature as it transitions between the seasons. The actual dates of these transitions shifted every few years, but the predictability of how the transformation occurred did not. It's usually around the end of March when residents began to get restless, hoping for a crocus or a daffodil to reveal their colorful bloom and break up the dismal and dirty snow and ice rejecting spring's overtures.

While the train headed northward, the students turned to their studies. Laptops were opened, books retrieved from backpacks and quiet enveloped the train. The only sound was that of the train on the tracks. As we rolled towards Saratoga Springs, I looked out the window at what was once land governed by a confederacy of indigenous nations known as the Iroquois Confederacy. This confederation of nations is said to have inspired many of the American colonists desiring a rupture from the British crown, but not a centralized government. Composed of the Cayuga, Mohawk, Oneida, Onondaga, Seneca and Tuscarora nations, these nations split their allegiances during the colonists' war for independence.

The Oneida and Tuscarora sided with the colonists, while the other four joined the British forces. Among other reasons, it was the British who had promised to leave them alone if they won the war. The American colonists had made it clear they had no plans to coexist with the indigenous nations. This is why the bulk of the nations of the Iroquois Confederation fought with the British. True to the Confederation's governance form, each nation was empowered to choose its own course. The power of the Iroquois was never as great after the victory of the colonists and the formation of the United States. The white man had done his job by dividing the Iroquois against themselves. Still, the nations remain. On occasion, they mount resistance to the intrusions of local, state and federal police forces. During the 1960s and into the 1970s, some members published one of the better underground papers called Akwesasne Notes. Like most conflicts the US authorities are involved in that involve other nations, the indigenous resistance usually involves issues of sovereignty. We all know that the sovereignty of indigenous nations has never been high on the list of things Washington and its subsidiary forces truly respect.

Several passengers left the train in Saratoga Springs. It seemed most were students at Skidmore College. Those of us remaining on the train were then able to spread out into the seats that were vacated. The weather outside remained cold and windy. I watched as snow flurries came and went outside my window. The forest was bare. Then I had another beer. While I drank it in the cafe car, I listened to a conversation between a middle-aged hetero couple sitting at the same table as me. They turned to me and asked my name. I told them and they shared their names and their story. From what I could gather, they had met at a classical music concert in Saratoga Springs a couple years previous. Both were rebounding from long term marriages that had dissolved without warning, at least from their perspectives. Now they were married, having tied the knot over the most recent winter holidays. Saratoga Springs was their romantic dinner, the renewal of their vows. All that good stuff that can happen to people in love. Of course, it does require a bit of forgetting to pull this off for a lifetime. I finished my beer, bought another and wished the two good luck before I headed back to my seat.

I was on my way to Minnesota. It was May 2023 and I was back on the Ethan Allen line. While I waited for the train in Burlington, Vermont, I thought about Ethan Allen. Good old Ethan. He was a tavern owner and a whiskey drinker who didn't want to pay taxes on the whiskey he sold. What is now Vermont was then part of New York. Ethan got together with several other like-minded individuals and they fomented a rebellion against the authorities who wanted to tax them. Vermont was its own independent nation for a little while. It ended up becoming the  fourteenth state of the rapidly centralizing federation known as the United States. In modern times Vermont has shown flashes of that former independence. First among those moments might be the civil union law for same sex couples. That recognition led to legalized marriage for same sex couples.

The train pulled into the Albany station. Albany is a typical US city in transition from its heady days as an industrial and transportation hub. At one time economically stable with decent unionized jobs, it now seems to be, at best, divided between working people

of fewer and fewer means and the moneyed class that feeds and feeds off the state and county bureaucracies located in the town. When one wanders downtown near the New York State capital building, one sees office buildings housing union bureaucracies. However, organized labor is not the power it was when Albany was an industrial and shipping hub. From what I could tell, some residential parts of town feature blocks full of boarded up row-houses and signs stating the properties are now owned by banks or a public-private mortgage trusts. In other words, gentrification is probably close at hand. One expects the owners of these properties see dollar signs, not people. Other residential sections seem to be doing just fine. However, in every section of the center city I rode or walked around in, I saw no supermarkets and very few bank branches. Several large banks do have buildings downtown. Everywhere else in this district, the only ATMs were those little portable ones you find in convenience stores. This means fee-less cash withdrawals are not convenient for most residents.

It's a little over a month since I took this line north from Albany.

The view from the train window was considerably greener. Maples and oaks were nearing full leafiness, and many of the aspen were already fully realized. Wildflowers populated the meadows, and farm animals were adjusting to the warmer temperatures. They weren't exactly luxuriating in them yet, but they were not huddled

together as they were on my previous passage through the north country. I imagine even the prisoners and guards in the numerous warehouses of humanity that exist in this area appreciated what sun they could see and feel.

However, some facts don't change no matter which direction one is headed in. Looking out the window, I saw hollowed-out warehouses and factories surrounded by hollowed-out towns. Capitalism almost always leaves destruction in its wake, and globalized capital has left a much wider scarring. The wealth it brought to the working people in the towns it invited itself into left when those towns and their people were used up. The only wealth that remains is in rich people's bank accounts. Most of those banks are international in their reach, which means the money they deal in goes where profit commands it to go, not where the money might help sustain a town and the people who live in it.

As the next train left Albany, a fellow was talking rather loudly on his cell phone when we were about ten minutes into the ride. The conversation continued for twenty more minutes, talking corporate deals. I guess he was hoping to hustle up his little piece of the pie. To avoid listening and getting annoyed, I plugged the Miles Davis soundscape known as *Live/Evil* into my ears. The train blew its horn every few seconds as we traveled along the line. The synergy between the music and the horn was seamless. Third generation trees of the upstate farmland rolled by, their shadows casting a stroboscopic sunlight on the train's interior. Small villages barely more than a crossroad or two went quickly past. Davis' urban fusion became a vision translating nature's seeming anarchy into a composition worthy of the forces expressed in both. As the evening faded into night, the towns and cities become little more than light. Inside the train, the only lights are dim ones in the ceiling illuminating the way through the cars, and those of passenger cell phones. Some are watching videos and some are playing games.

By the time I awoke shortly after dawn, the train was chugging through Ohio. It slowed down as we headed into Toledo. A massive grain storage facility sat near the river. It was obvious that the passenger train station once contained four tracks, but was now down to only one, its weather-beaten signs and battered benches reflecting the forlornness of the place; all of this enhanced by the fact it looked like it hadn't been painted in years. I couldn't help

think of the station's condition as symbolic of a state where money has been removed from the public coffers and put into the bank accounts of the best-off. As we moved out of Toledo and on into the Ohio countryside I saw massive fields, recently plowed, anticipating their summer growth. Occasional birds perched on the small trees and bushes that separate the railroad tracks from the fields. Whippoorwills, maybe bobwhites.

As the train moved into Indiana, warehouses stood along the track, their lots filled with goods. RVs, axles, short buses, and passenger vans. I noticed deserted and overgrown track running parallel to the track we were on, situated closer to the warehouses. No longer in use, it remained from the days when most freight in the United States was transported by train. Freight cars had been loaded directly from the warehouses along the track siding, and eventually hitched to an engine. Now, the tractor trailers in the warehouse parking lots do the hauling.

Not long after I noticed the warehouses and abandoned railroad track, the train stopped in Elkhart, Indiana. A couple dozen Amish men, women and children boarded. One of them, named Marlon, sat down next to me. At first, he conversed in Dutch with his wife and daughter who sat in the seats across the aisle. Then, after everyone in his party was settled in their seats, he turned to me and asked me where I was traveling from. I told him I'd been on the train since Vermont and our conversation began. Over the course of the hour or two we spent talking it came up that I used to hitchhike a fair amount in the 1970s and the early 1980s. Marlon was intrigued, wondering about this aspect of car culture. After all, being Amish, it was a culture he had no familiarity with. His mode of transportation was and is a horse and buggy. I told him a couple of stories and answered his questions. I then shifted the conversation to his community. Beyond the religious and historical elements of the Amish, I knew very little about how they actually made their living in an outside economy that emphasized money over all else. He told me that many of the younger men in the settlements he was associated with in the region of Indiana we were passing through worked at the RV factories I mentioned previously. As they got older and developed skills, most men moved into some kind of self-employment. Marlon made cupboards and bureaus. He continued, telling me that layoffs during and since the pandemic had effected the economies of the settlements, forcing many of the laid-off fellows to take their gardening and farming more seriously. As Marlon explained it, this wasn't necessarily to their liking. It was much harder work.

The community he described was both a millenarian and simple response to a world growing ever more commercial and crass. It provided some comfort and consistency in its insularity and its rules. This didn't mean it was an easy life, nor that it was without the temptations the world holds. We looked around the train car, noticing the number of passengers looking at their phones. Marlon remarked that this phone fascination was a problem with the young people in his community, too. It was an interesting contradiction, is how he described it. Buggies and cell phones.

The impulse towards community that came through in my conversation with Marlon is obviously not unique to religious groups. While remembering my exchange with this Amish man, I recalled a talk I had helped organize in Burlington, Vermont a couple of months earlier. The featured speaker was a fellow residing in Jackson, Mississippi named Kali Akuno. The community he helped found is known as Cooperation Jackson. Essentially an autonomous collective of people fighting the white supremacist regime of Mississippi's state government, it is a collection of people working to inform and organize the economically and racially marginalized people of Mississippi. Its commitment is to a mutual aid framework that includes and incorporates the people it is assisting while simultaneously educating themselves. While Kali discussed the project with the assembled audience at the event, I was reminded of the survival activities undertaken by the Black Panther Party — breakfast programs, anti-colonial schools, etc. In short, the goal of this and other such organizations is to create a dual power that by its actions challenges the existing (and colonial) state. Like the Amish, who have their origins in opposition to the Catholic church, the nobility and the wars of both, Cooperation Jackson is a phenomenon that hopes and tries to exist outside of the oppressive regime the rulers call democracy. Because of its overtly political (not religious) philosophy, it seems clear that it will remain a target of that democracy's forces of law and order. Similarly, if one reads the histories of some of the Protestant sects of the radical reformation from which the Amish developed, they will find that those sects were also attacked and even destroyed by the power of the wealthy, the Church and their armies.

I switched trains in Chicago. Unlike my last time here in March, the downtown was open for business. After orienting myself, I left Union Station and headed into the sunny, windy streets. I was looking for some decent food and cheaper alcohol than what was available on the train. As I walked down Clinton Street, the sun shone brightly, the high-rises casting their shadows while the traffic did its dance from stoplight to stoplight. A few blocks away from the station, I found an Asian supermarket, and wandered through the aisles looking for something both tasty and easy to eat. I settled on a package of spicy fish, vegetables and noodles. I supplemented the food with a liter of mango nectar and a couple of ten ounce containers of saki. I looked for a place to sit down and eat, and found a small park across from a Catholic church named after Saint Patrick. As I ate, I watched several young, well-dressed individuals walk their dogs through the park, cleaning up their waste after the animals deposited it. I'm guessing the humans were on a lunch break. They all seemed to be in a hurry. Their dogs seemed resigned to the fact that this walk was little more than a bathroom break. None of them dawdled at trees to sniff and fret. It was all business. The sun felt good and the fresh air was a pleasant change from the train's canned atmosphere. I put the saki in my pack, saving it for later. By the time I got back to the station I had a little more than an hour to wait for my train to Minneapolis. I ended up talking with a guy coming back from West Virginia on his way to Traverse City, Michigan. After he told me he had forgotten he had a bag of marijuana in his knapsack and only remembered when he was halfway to West Virginia, we discussed the fact that marijuana was still illegal in West Virginia. He laughed, saying his friends in Morgantown were happy he had spaced out the fact he had the weed. He remarked that it was weird to be paranoid about possessing weed after living in a place like Michigan, where it was legal. I concurred, remembering the first couple of weeks after it was legalized in Vermont. The paranoia I was used to after the first toke hit the brain took a few weeks before it no longer occurred. Now, it's no different than drinking a beer in terms of being afraid the cops are watching and waiting.

My train was announced, and I headed to the track as instructed. The train was called the Empire Builder. When I heard that, I laughed at the imperial audacity of the title. We left on time. Soon we were in Wisconsin, many of its fields partially submerged after a week of rain. I glimpsed a heron swallowing a frog in a flooded creek near the track, and saw a school bus re-fabricated to look like a rocket ship submerged in a muddy field. When we arrived in Milwaukee, I was surprised at the number of new buildings downtown. I hadn't been in the state since 1987 when my friend Holly and I traveled across country with one of my brothers and our then three-year old son. I was amused to see that the Wisconsin Dells

were still the geological mystery I always found them to be, and that the kitschy commercialization of them was pretty much as I remembered it. The fact that the state's politics were now a right-wing disaster was not apparent from the train window. However, I knew better. The destruction of the social fabric begun under the rule of Scott Walker had changed some of my Wisconsin friends' lives in ways they were still recovering from. Some had lost their jobs, while many more found themselves wondering how long their jobs would be worth keeping, what with the growing number of restrictions regarding classroom curricula being made into law. Two men in the seats directly in front of me discussed the merits of McDonald's versus Arby's. I didn't feel qualified to join the conversation, but could not help overhearing it. Despite the involved conversation (or perhaps because it was so involved) there was no final consensus. Eventually, one of them fell asleep and the other went back to playing video games on his device.

Crossing the state line into Minnesota always reminds me of my childhood. Both of my parents were from the Twin Cities. I was born in Minneapolis. We began the life of a transient military family before I turned one year old. My father's first assignment was San Antonio, Texas. Then a couple places in Alaska. Then we went to Maryland, followed by Pakistan. When I was younger, my mom and dad would pack us into the family station wagon a couple of times a year and we would drive from Maryland to Minnesota stopping overnight in Ohio, and staying at a roadside motel. The rides were what one would expect in a family vacation. Some boredom, a grumpy dad driving, roadside sandwiches and KoolAid, and a lot of reading and I Spy types of games. Dad's grumpiness increased when the weather was hot. After all, cars didn't have air conditioning back then and driving long distances is hard work for most folks.

The Indiana Turnpike always interested me, its Howard Johnson restaurants located on walkways across the road connecting the two rest stops present. Our reward was all the time spent with grandparents, cousins and the rest of the extended family. Occasionally, we actually stopped at one of those Howard Johnson's, and my parents bought each of us an ice cream cone. Their numerous flavors of ice cream was one of the restaurant's selling points. I worked at a Howard Johnson's in Maryland for a few months in 1976. The manager was the son of the owner of the franchise. Most of my co-workers in the kitchen were Black and older than the manager and me. The manager insisted we call him Mister M — . We refused and continued to just call him by his surname. When he wasn't calling them boy, he called the Black men by their first name. The waitresses and the bartender were mostly young, attractive single white women. A couple of the servers who worked breakfast and lunch were married. The local cops hung out at the place way too much for my comfort. They flirted with the waitresses and got their meals and drinks free. One evening, the oldest cook called in sick because his youngest child was at the emergency room in the closest hospital, about fifteen miles away. Mr. M — started yelling at him over the phone, telling him he had an hour to get to work or he would be fired. I hated the job and didn't give a shit whether or not I kept it. After he slammed down the phone, Mr. M — came into the galley and told me I would be cooking alone because he had just fired that damn n****r cook who acted like he ran the joint. I finished the orders I had begun, looked at Mr. M — and took off my hat and apron. I laughed and told him I was sick of his racist bullshit and was quitting. He started yelling and I yelled back. Then I left...quickly. The dishwashers followed me. Howard Johnson's mailed me my last paycheck.

In later years, a couple of my sisters moved to Minnesota. Whenever I passed over the gorge at the Wisconsin-Minnesota border just beyond LaCrosse, Wisconsin I was amazed at its beauty. It was in the early 1980s when I traveled that trail the most. Micky, the sister I was on my way to see this journey, lived in Rochester while the other lived north of the Twin Cities. I was on a highway ramp near the Heileman Brewery in LaCrosse. The brewery was just beginning its drive to be one of the largest in the United States. It wasn't doing this by brewing more beer, but by buying out other brewers, selling off their equipment, and often laying off the workers. It was a Sunday morning, and I was heading towards Rochester, where my sister lived about twenty feet from a tavern called the North Star. Taverns and now brewpubs were (and still are) a big deal in Minnesota, serving as communal spaces and getaways in a way unlike most other places I've been, kind of like the gasthauses were in Germany when I lived there. My sister spent nights at the North Star when she wasn't working at the state hospital. She was a reigning pool shark. When she was on her game and playing for pitchers of beer, we never spent a nickel on beer. A chapter of one of the local biker clubs hung out there. Her pool playing had gained their respect. Once a member told me that part of the initiation process for potential members involved trying to beat Micky at the table. He might have been pulling my leg, but it was a good story and added to her legend there.

Anyhow, I was standing on the ramp with my thumb out. A brewery worker had dropped me off there on his way to work. I had some marijuana stashed carefully in my backpack, which rested next to me on the shoulder of the road. The day was warming up quickly. A Wisconsin state trooper pulled his car up in front of me and got out. As he approached, he asked me for identification. I took my wallet out of my jeans pocket and my ID out of my wallet. He took it back to the car and called in my information. I waited. After about five minutes and some back and forth between the trooper and a dispatcher, he came back to where I was standing, handed me my ID and asked me where I was heading. I told him to Rochester to visit my sister. We made small talk for a few minutes. I relaxed and so did he. He told me he had a cousin who worked at the same hospital as my sister. We talked about my trip so far, and then he wished me luck. By the time we were done conversing I had almost forgotten about the very illegal stash I had in my pack. I got a ride straight through to Rochester only minutes after the trooper left, with a woman on her way to the Mayo Clinic for a stay. Her cancer treatment required a visit to the Clinic every few weeks. I was impressed by her positive attitude.

Now, in 2023, there are still a few Trump flags flying in these parts. It's like they know their battle isn't over. If it was and they had won it all, flying their flag might be mandatory. It would be like any other authoritarian in the middle of their reign erecting statues of themselves in parks and town squares. The presence of these flags indicate a belief trumpism has yet to die its final death. Only time will tell.

The train crossed the Mississippi about ten miles south of where the Interstate 94 bridge is. The Mississippi was over its usual banks, but still safely within the flood plain. The setting sun shone like an orange ball through the trees, its glow reflected in the river waters. Lake Onalaska was over its banks, too, its still waters disturbed only by someone fishing here and there. The sight was as breathtaking as I remembered it. As the train headed north and west, I watched the sky turn from day to darkness. The beauty of this transition seemed to silence the car as the passengers looked quietly out their windows. We were once again reminded that no human-made spectacle comes close to the beauty nature often reveals, no matter how much money was spent.

Writing about my dad reminds me of his dying. It's trite to say, but it's weird to watch someone fade before your eyes. This occurred with my mom and my dad ten years apart. The body returns to the dust they say from whence it came. Memories remain. Some were renewed as the months dwindled to weeks and finally to days and hours. After all, it's the time people spent together that makes their lives mean something to each other. The fact we moved every two or three years — often to another country — gave me my love of travel and desire to experience what was previously unknown to me.

Family is how I keep time. Its existence, and the continuation through generations reminds me of our temporality. I see my older sister retire, her hair graying and then I look in the mirror and see this older visage in my reflection. My son and his cousins fall in love once, twice maybe more until they discover the one who they hope they will stay with. Children come, their innocence reflected in their faces and antics a pleasant reminder of the nature of time, humanity and more. Given that most of my relatives still live in Minnesota, there were bound to be some family get-togethers on this trip. After getting off the train, my sister Micky and I found each other outside the station, and went to her house north of the Twin Cities. On the way, she told me which relatives we would be visiting. The next day, we headed out on one of those visits. My father's brother, Jim, and his wife Louise, would be our hosts. Another uncle, several cousins and some of their children were present. The occasion was Mother's Day. The conversations were animated, multi-generational, and included topics spanning family updates to politics and the future. To my relief, Trump was mentioned only in the past tense at this gathering. In fact, I met no one on this journey who supported him.

We also visited one of my mother's sisters — my godmother in fact. She lived closer to Minneapolis, but still not in what one

might call the old city. As we drove through that section of the city, my sister and I talked about the last time she had been in Minneapolis proper. She was attending a solidarity protest with Minnesota nurses on strike. Prior to that visit, she had been at a couple of actions after the murder of George Floyd by Minneapolis police officers. That protest was also one called by the nurses' union — Minnesota Nurses Association.

My cousin Katie, an environmental activist who has begun to include indigenous rights in her campaigns, told me the train I had been on went within a couple hundred meters of a gardening project she was involved in. If I remember correctly, the plot was on disputed land next to (or possibly on) land ceded to the Dakota/Mdewakanton people. The Prairie Island nuclear power plant is in the same area. It stores its spent fuel in casks buried in the ground. As one can imagine, this has resulted in higher than ordinary cancer rates for the people who live in the area, especially the native peoples.

Katie also said the payments to the communities in the plant's vicinity vary according to whether or not the population is white or native. As in other parts of the country where indigenous people constitute a sizable part of the population, the history of land appropriation by the white folks moving into the area is very much a fact. At the same time, there is now a casino on the Goodhue reservation land that has helped the indigenous community provide good medical care, better educational opportunities and helped create a rebirth of Mdewakanton and Dakota Sioux culture. The bluff where an influential elder is buried is named after the white man who acquired the land. That bluff is under dispute now, as the Mdewakanton and their allies are fighting to reclaim and rename it. During our conversation, she mentioned that the train stopped in Red Wing, just up the road from where she lived. This brought up the song "The Walls of Red Wing" by Bob Dylan. As she read the lyrics aloud, my relatives corrected the misconceptions presented therein. I suggested that Dylan was merely using poetic license when he sang that the prison, which ran on an honor system, had walls. We agreed that Dylan was allowed a bit of poetic license. After all, he was Bob Dylan.

My dad's father worked in the Grain Belt brewery as a steamfitter. I remember Grain Belt beer being present at every family party in Minnesota back in my youth. Brewery workers were provided with a case of beer every week. The beer was fine but the bottles were mislabeled on these cases, which meant they weren't going to be sold to the public. Grain Belt brewery was bought out in the 1980s by a larger brewery, which then broke the union, cut back production and destroyed the brand. It was classic capitalist behavior that became standard during Ronald Reagan's morning in America. A couple of decades later, a small brewery bought the Grain Belt recipe and began producing the beer again. It is a regional favorite once more. Speaking of beer, it seems safe to say that Minnesotans still like their barley. My sister and I hit up two brewpubs within ten miles of her house in rural Minnesota. The brews were tasty and both were quite busy. We conversed with a few folks enjoying their weekend, the sunshine and the brew.

As in so much of the United States, the abuse of narcotics and methamphetamine has reached crisis proportions in Minnesota. My sister, a psychiatric nurse, works in an addiction treatment clinic. As you might guess, she has a multitude of stories to tell about her daily work. The doctor who works with her seems like a compassionate soul who rejects judging those who use the clinic's services. Of course, not everyone who works at these kinds of places is non-judgmental. Some approach it as missionary work, hoping to save souls. Others grow cynical, forgetting the motivation that brought them to the clinics in the first place. That cynicism can breed a contempt for the patients these people see. Nonetheless, something in their being compels them to work there.

The epidemic of addictive drugs in the US says a lot about the culture we exist in, revealing that culture's crude commercialism and its focus on self-gratification. Even more than either of those, it reveals the hopelessness of vast numbers of US residents, who see no real future for themselves. When so much of one's existence requires money and its pursuit, why spend whatever cash one has on anything but a guaranteed blank bliss, a high that transcends reality's ugliness and despair? Religion doesn't work for everyone as a way to justify their otherwise treadmill existence. Politics only breeds cynicism in a culture so tainted by money, and love is all too often just another commercial venture. Addicts are the canaries in the coal mine of a system spiraling downward. They are also the seeds left in dirt that nurtures nothing. The few who benefit from this destructive, broken system have no compassion, and will be recognized as the agents of capital they truly are when the history of this moment is recalled down the road. That is, if there's anyone left to recall it accurately.

On my previous visits, Florida seemed a place where humanity's better attributes were slowly being destroyed and hardly anyone living there gave a shit. Now, the reality is that the destruction has quickened, and a substantial proportion of the population is cheering the process on.

I hate to think this is the future of the United States. Right now, I would say it can go either way. My guess is as good as yours at this point. I feel bad for the kids. I could go on about the attacks on people's sexuality, their skin tone, and their politics undertaken by the government of Florida. I could talk about the transfer of control of educational institutions to the right-wing government and the various religious and political organizations that advise it. Likewise, I could talk about laws that essentially deny the humanity of non-heterosexual individuals, while giving everyone and their children the right to own a gun and use it to defend whatever they consider to be their ground to stand on. But, why bother? You get my drift and you are probably aware of the politics of Florida. It's hard to believe it was once a state governed by relatively liberal politicians. Then again, it's hard to believe that politicians like Joe Biden and Hillary Clinton are considered progressive. Of course, the governor of Florida and his supporters probably consider both of them to be communists.

A bulletin from the NAACP showed up in my social media a couple of weeks before I got on the plane to Tampa. It read, in part, "WARNING! The NAACP Board of Directors has issued a formal travel advisory for the state of Florida. "Florida is openly hostile toward African Americans, people of color and LGBTQ+ individuals," the notice states. "Before traveling to Florida, please understand that the state of Florida devalues and marginalizes the contributions of, and the challenges faced by African Americans and other communities of color." A friend of mine who was teaching at the New College in Sarasota lost his job after the state government replaced the board of trustees with a collection of right wing religious zealots, and a couple plain old fascists. Prior to the takeover of the college, New College was a progressive and cutting-edge school. It is now a tool of the most reactionary forces in the state. Rick Scott, a hateful, pompous and crooked politician who used to be Florida's governor and now represents them in the Senate, released his own warning in response to the NAACP one. His release told socialists that Florida was openly hostile to them. I suppose it was meant as a joke, but I never really got frat-boy humor or its adult equivalent at the country club.

There's an agenda touted by the ultra-right in the United States known as the Florida blueprint. In short, the Florida blueprint is a blueprint for fascism. The possibility of it going national is both scary and possible. In essence, it pretends to be for small government, and against big corporations and banks, but in reality it wants to increase the government's intrusion into people's personal lives while giving supportive corporations and financial houses more control of the economy. The former is done by passing laws regarding individual gender and sexual choices and women's reproductive rights. The latter is achieved by removing environmental and labor regulations and minimizing other government controls on excess profiteering, while reducing taxes on the corporations and the wealthy. In addition, white supremacist practices are encouraged and supported by everything from the removal of laws preventing discrimination based on skin tone to the drastic revision of school curricula and the censorship of school textbooks. The latter usually involves removing mentions of slavery, Jim Crow, police brutality and other obvious elements of racial apartheid in the United States. It is a scenario both frightening and possible, with Florida being a prime example.

So yeah, this journey to Florida was made with greater trepidation than previous ones. It was not only a journey to a right-wing wasteland, it was a journey to a dystopia that is both modern and retro, authoritarian and chaotic, with a future taken from the Book of Revelations as a video game. Is what I am seeing really real or can I just use my controller to go to another level where all the klansmen, Nazis and their cheerleaders are either not allowed, or easier to dispense with? The hell I had entered was obvious before I left the Tampa airport. An advertisement on a wall reminded travelers that Ron Desantis was the governor in the so-called sunshine state. His dream is to bring his laws of fear to the nation, where swimsuit beauty pageants will replace drag queen story times. He and his followers don't seem to have enough room in their brains for both existing simultaneously.

Florida is one of those places where I never completely relax in public. Between the police, the plethora of motor vehicles, and the inhospitable architecture, a part of me is always on edge. My inability to truly chill out was exacerbated on this visit to DeSantisized Florida. Despite the politics, I still dug the warm weather and my hosts. The natural beauty that still exists in the area north of Tampa where I was staying is most unlike that which I've seen in the previous journeys in this book. Crystal clear rivers, Spanish moss, mangrove trees and scrub pines are quite a statement when contrasted to the sandy backyards where Floridians waste water on lawns which would brown overnight without it. One can almost forget the suburban streets as wide and straight as any in California's Orange County when they look down into the waters where manatees pod in the Florida spring. The brash commercialism of the culture is no different than that found in so much of this country where people congregate. However, the joyful acceptance of it in Florida may be unmatched.

After picking up a rental car at the Tampa airport — an experience in itself for me since I don't drive and therefore rarely spend time at a rental car outlet — my friend Holly and I headed out to the highway. We went perhaps thirty miles on a toll road called Veterans' Highway. What can I say about the worship veterans get in this country other than it's both ridiculous and counterfeit. Highways and parks are named in their memory while unhoused veterans fighting emotional and mental demons linked to the wars they were sent to fight stand at highway exits begging for food and work. Older men wearing baseball hats with the name of the ship or the unit they were assigned to salute each other at flea markets where they sell things to supplement their disability checks. If by chance, a veteran publicly opposes the next war and regrets their fighting an earlier one, their status goes almost immediately from hero to traitor among the politicians and corporate slime whose bank accounts hide the money they get from the bloody deeds of empire.

Three or four blocks after we exited the highway we rode by a protest by a group calling themselves Moms for Liberty. They seemed to be protesting a store's selling clothing celebrating LBGT+ during the corporate-dominated holiday of Pride Month. Besides the obvious contradiction of Moms touting liberty while demanding a store curtail its freedom to sell stuff, I couldn't help wonder why these women got so worked up about humans and their sexual attractions. I also wondered how many of the rank and file Moms for Liberty knew they were being manipulated by corporations and corporate churches into hating things that could someday result in them hating their children or grandchildren.

One of the roads we crossed on our way to our destination is called Cortez Boulevard. Unlike other places I've visited this past year, Florida seems to be perfectly fine with its invaders' legacy. Not that Cortez had much to do with Florida, but the fact that this street had never been renamed says a lot about the state's history involving non-white people. Indeed, the water now known as Tampa Bay once housed indigenous people known as the Tocobaga. A peaceful people, they lived off the plentiful wildlife on both the land and in the sea. Around 1528, Spanish invaders under the leadership of Pánfilo de Narváez, landed in the bay. They brought disease and violence to the area. Within one hundred years, the Tocobaga were extinct.

Once we reached our destination, our hosts took us to a restaurant. It had been more than eight hours since Holly and I had eaten anything but airplane pretzels. While we drank a couple of beers, I couldn't help overhearing a very loud middle-aged woman in a nearby booth talking about the unhoused. Her whining grew louder as she described a man who was panhandling in front of a store she frequented. Her description, which made the poor fellow into something barely human, revealed a pathological hatred for poor people. She and her party left soon afterwards. They got into a 2023 Cadillac sedan and drove off. She was driving. Our server took the tip from that table, brought us a new round of beers and whispered she was glad to see them go.

Although I didn't do a lot of wandering during my Florida visit, I did notice a few clothing trends in the restaurants and shops. I had spotted these trends elsewhere in the United States but, as I said before, everything seems more concentrated in Florida. About a third of the people seemed to dress as if they were at a country music concert, wearing cut-offs and heels or cowboy boots; older folks tended to wear gaudy shirts and shorts, and way too many young white guys dressed like frat boys at a summertime kegger, their shorts and tank tops often matching and occasionally bearing advertisements for beer or professional sports teams.

I don't want to be too politically specific here, but I do have to say that Florida seems a meaner place than it was before the Trump presidency. There were always lots of right-leaning folks in the part of the state I have visited most often, but their presence did not dominate as it seems to now. The lack of compassion combined with the arrogance of certain older white Americans and right-wing immigrants has been manipulated into a political movement that looks forward to a country free of the likes of people like me. That in itself has some problems in general, but it is the parts of the past this loud (and racist) minority champions — racial and gender intolerance — that shows the true nature of the politicians riding these sentiments to power. Indeed, while I was there, a new anti-immigrant law took effect, provoking protests by immigrants, employers and the seemingly small percentage of Floridians who are not part of the reactionary tide or believe they are immune from it.

My trip to Florida seems like the appropriate place to mention the fact of climate change. Like millions of others not tied to a politics that requires denial or doomsaying, I find myself wondering what the hell is going on when a deep freeze hits New England weeks later than such a freeze usually occurred thirty years ago when I first moved to Vermont. Likewise, while I wandered the trails of Folsom, California with my brother in January 2023, both of us couldn't help but comment on how cold the temperature was for that part of California. At the same time, the newspapers were filled with stories of the torrential rains along the California coast. I have to admit that when the New England summer extends itself into late September I am a happy man, walking by the river while I remember sub-freezing nights at the same time in the calendar thirty years ago. Without having any knowledge of the weather beyond being able to guess when a storm might be coming, and what I've learned from watching and reading weather reports over the past decades, it's clear that the climate is changing. It seems equally clear that this is in some way related to human industrial activity and its products. It is also pretty clear that certain powerful humans don't care about this and that even more from all walks of life don't know what to do about it. Needless to say, it was hot in Florida. While I was there, a man on the news said over 300, 000 people moved there in 2022. That sounds like the combination of the greater heat and the growing population is a recipe for some kind of catastrophe.

Well, there you have it. These journeys took me to a number of places, allowed me to interact with people and provided me with views beautiful and not so beautiful. Some of the conversations were with old friends and some were with strangers who will remain so. Future journeys will continue as long as my feet can carry me. I reject the idea of making some grand statement about the state of this nation other then the one implied in the title of this work. There's a lot of desperation and unnecessary poverty that is combined with (and related to) the arrogance and the stupidity of wealth. And still people are trying to keep the fires going, looking for love and celebrating the ones they have.

The scars from recessions and depressions remain across the land'. Sections of many cities are little more than hollowed-out buildings waiting for capitalism's next short term investments, always promising rebirth and riches. Even though we've been sold this line before, politicians and bureaucratic hacks will do what it takes to sell it to the voters while pocketing their cut. Everywhere one goes, there are people who can't afford to rent a place to live. Too many end up incarcerated. The rest are living and working in the fields, farms and orchards of the nation, the strip malls all over the USA, the hollowed-out buildings of the cities and in the streets themselves. Those who have a house or two are often quick to blame the poor for their poverty, calling on the gods they've created in their own image for affirmation of their fear and hatred. The Jesus I once read about weeps, wondering how his command to love thy neighbors as yourself became so twisted. Too many preach hate in his name. Perhaps it's time for those who do so to suffer for their sins. If I'm being brutally honest, I have to admit I hope that's the case.

I remain convinced that the future will feature greater cruelty and despair unless the pursuit of profit is removed from human exchange. It doesn't matter how many good people there are when the greediest among us can profit from our work and our despair. When that greed is encouraged by the methods with which we conduct business, the human spirit is turned from one which celebrates life to one that celebrates things. It is a turn which bodes ill for life. It is also a trajectory that will require an incredible struggle to change.

Acknowledgments

First and foremost, I want to thank those who hosted me during the journeys I took while writing this book. My family in Maryland, especially my sister Kathy; my brother Tim and his wife Mary Beth in Folsom, California; and my daughter Hannah and her household, my son Ian and his family in Maine and Rhode Island, respectively. Similarly, I can't thank my friends Stephanie and Andy in Portland and Olympia enough. The same goes for David and Agustina in Austin. Lastly, but certainly not least, I want to thank my sister Micky in Minnesota.

Next, I am exceedingly grateful to everyone who contributed to my request for funds to finance these trips. My appreciation for your assistance is immeasurable.

Once again, thanks goes out to the awesome duo of Donna Bister and Marc Estrin at Fomite Books. Their commitment to publishing is beyond remarkable and deserves considerably more plaudits than I can give here.

Fomite

Writing a review on social media sites for readers will help the progress of independent publishing. To submit a review, go to the book page on any of the sites and follow the links for reviews. Books from independent presses rely on reader-to-reader communications.

For more information or to order any of our books, visit:
fomitepress.com/our-books.html

More essays from Fomite...

William Benton — *Eye Contact: Writing on Art*

J. Malcom Garcia — *A Different Kind of War: Uneasy Encounters in Mexico and Central America*

Stephen Langfur — *Confession from a Jericho Jail*

Douglas W. Milliken — *Any Less You*

George Ovitt & Peter Nash — *Trotsky's Sink: Ninety-Eight Short Essays on Literature*

Robert Sommer — *Losing Francis: Essays on the Wars at Home*

Made in United States
Troutdale, OR
05/11/2024

19817247R00087